K 1942

WHY THE CHURCH MUST TEACH

Lucien E. Coleman, Jr.

BROADMAN PRESS
Nashville, Tennessee

Unless otherwise stated, all Scripture quotations are from the
Revised Standard Version of the Bible, copyrighted 1946, 1952,
© 1971, 1973.
Scripture quotations marked KJV are from the King James Version
of the Bible.
Scripture quotations marked NIV are from HOLY BIBLE *New
International Version,* copyright © 1978, New York Bible Society.
Used by permission.
Scripture quotations marked GNB are from the *Good News Bible,*
the Bible in Today's English Version. Old Testament: Copyright ©
American Bible Society 1976; New Testament: Copyright ©
American Bible Society 1966, 1971, 1976. Used by permission.

Library of Congress Cataloging in Publication Data

Coleman, Lucien E.
  Why the Church must teach.

  1. Christian education. 2. Church–Teaching
office. I. Title.
BV1471.2.C634 1984   207   84-4966
ISBN 0-8054-3234-5

To Bobbie
With whom and from whom
I have learned in the Lord

Contents

Foreword

This is a book about the teaching ministry of the church. As such, it grapples with one of the profoundest issues in contemporary life, namely, the breakdown of that educative process by which the accumulated wisdom and values of the centuries are transmitted to each new generation.

Consider the near collapse of the teaching task in American society today. Electoral politics once provided a forum which allowed candidates to clarify for the public the great issues of state. As recently as the 1950s, Adlai Stevenson set out to "talk sense" to the American people in a series of major policy statements, but after the Kennedy-Nixon television debates of 1960, campaigning quickly degenerated into "image-building" through symbols and slogans devoid of substance. Ironically, the mass media have never been more technologically proficient at communicating through both sight and sound, yet they have virtually abandoned the educational function in favor of a mindless entertainment that neither instructs nor inspires. Even our newspapers are in retreat from the type of reflective journalism practiced by Walter Lippman which prompted a wider populace to ponder the deeper implications of current events. Instead, didactic analysis has been replaced by "human interest features" designed to compete with the impresssionistic style of the television talk-shows.

There was a time when music, especially the great oratorios, taught us the archetypal stories of mankind, but now we cannot even understand the words—and would not know what they meant if we could! There was a time when art depicted the great events of history on canvas or in stone, but now, in its more abstract expression, it strives to evoke a feeling which in itself has no content. There was a time when the home was the central learning center of the race, but now the last persons that many children would turn to for tutelege are their oft-absent parents. In their defense, most conscientious parents hope that the schools will provide the kind of training that was done in the home as recently as a century ago, but a host of prestigious experts report that the quality of teaching in our schools has actually declined rather than improved in recent years (cf. the Report of the National Commission on Excellence in Education, 1983). None of this is a nostalgic lament for a bygone era. Rather, it is a warning cry that we are facing a major crisis precisely at the point of Lucien Coleman's central concern in this book.

The church is not immune to the "de-educationalization" of American life hinted at above. On every hand its teaching minstry is under subtle if not frontal attack. There are some who emphasize evangelism so exclusively that no time or energy is left to concentrate on the nurture that should follow an initial decision for Christ. Others take a more avowedly anti-intellectual stance, attacking even Christian colleges and seminaries for fostering a climate of free inquiry where objections may be raised to traditional orthodoxy. Because education itself has become controversial in some quarters, many pastors try to sidestep the issue by majoring on the therapeutic side of ministry. Gilbert Highet, himself a master teacher, has commented insightfully on how this compartmentalization cannot be maintained:

> A minister of God can do a great deal by merely being there. Company is sympathy. . . . But after silent sympathy has done all it can, consolation still has to be given in words. If these words are to have any permanent effect, they must have some content. What content can they have, except advice, explanation, teaching? The Christian church has been best in those periods when it took its mission of teaching most seriously, and its priests still show their noblest side when they teach us how to bear what must be borne.[1]

At bottom, teaching is an essential ministry of the church for at least two reasons. First, it is inevitable because of the human thirst for meaning to which Highet has just alluded. Even in tragedy, people yearn for some understanding of what is happening to them. Second, it is indispensable because Christianity is an historical religion. That is, our Faith has a proper content which consists primarily of the saving acts of God among his people, supremely in the ministry of Jesus Christ. There is simply no way for a believing community to appropriate this content, which is found in a library of sixty-six sacred books written during more than a thousand years on more than a thousand pages, except by a continuous and competent process of instruction. Clear proof that "the church must teach" is provided by the fact that, when it fails to do so, false teachings rush in to fill the vacuum. The key issue, therefore, is not *whether* we shall teach but *how* we may do so effectively.

In addressing that issue, there is one major problem to be overcome which is widely recognized but seldom discussed. The rapid growth of religious education in recent years has tended to create a separate specialty in our seminaries designed to train persons for a separate vocation in our churches. The drive to give a clear identity to this specialization has served, perhaps unwittingly, to drive a cleft between the more "classical" and the more "practical" sides of our Faith which did not exist in the New Testament churches. As a result, there are many Biblical and theological specialists today who know very little about religious education and seem to disdain it almost as an alien enterprise. Likewise, there are religious educators so caught up in the practicalities of church programming that they seem to lack Biblical and theological depth, implying by their priorities that methods rather than content matter most.

The great value of all Lucien Coleman's writings, and especially of this book, is that he combines these two separated and sometimes antagonistic disciplines in equal balance. Those concerned for classical foundations will find that he knows the scriptural material thoroughly and has studied it with the help of the best biblical scholarship. Likewise, those concerned for practical application will find that he is equally at home in a contemporary Sunday School class and has mastered the learning theory needed to undergird a program of lay religious education in the local church. In fact, it would be hard to think of anyone among Southern Baptists who possesses more competence to mediate between these two fields which are so vital to each other but which often have only a nodding acquaintance.

Therefore, I commend a close study of Coleman's book by both pastor and minister of education alike. I urge group study by the educational leaders in local churches who desire excellence in the teaching ministry of their congregations. Finally, I appeal for denominational workers and seminarians to make this book the basis for fresh dialogue especially between those concerned primarily for biblical integrity and those concerned primarily for programmatic effectiveness. My prayer is that all who read these pages will do so in the spirit of Colossians 1:28-29.[2]

> This is the Christ we proclaim; we train everyone and teach everyone the full scope of this knowledge, in order to set everyone before God mature in Christ; I labour for that end, striving for it with the divine energy which is a power within me.

WILLIAM E. HULL
First Baptist Church
Shreveport, Louisiana

Notes

1. Gilbert Highet, *The Art of Teaching* (New York: Knopf, 1950), pp. 269-270.
2. From *The Bible: a New Translation* by James A. R. Moffatt. Copyright © 1935 by Harper and Row, Publishers, Inc. Used by permission.

Preface

Early in my career as a religious educator I came across a small volume, *The Recovery of the Teaching Ministry,* written by a Canadian Presbyterian minister, J. Stanley Glen. On the first page of that book, I found these words:

> In spite of the traditional emphasis that the church has placed on catechetical instruction and the education of its ministry, as well as the emphasis it has placed on its Sunday Schools and the movement represented by them, a strange subordination of the teaching function pervades its life, work, worship, and proclamation. The subordination is not a surface phenomenon due only to limitations at the administrative level, but a spiritual phenomenon due to a deeper, underlying condition, which robs the teaching ministry of its power and obstructs it in relation to the constitutive source of faith.[1]

Something within me responded to those words. I felt that Glen had put his finger on a fundamental problem within contemporary Christianity.

At first glance, it might seem that education is prospering in today's churches. We spend big money on educational facilities, publish an awesome array of curriculum materials, and enlist thousands of men and women to serve as leaders in teaching and training programs. But, just beneath the surface, there are indications that the teaching ministry is regarded as a secondary and, in some instances, nonessential function of the church.

Consider, for example, the stringent time limits imposed upon Bible study in most churches. The typical Sunday morning schedule allocates sixty to seventy-five minutes to Sunday School. Seldom more. But, the time spent in Bible study is drastically reduced by a variety of factors, including chronic tardiness on the part of members, opening programs, coffee fellowships, announcements, record taking, and various promotional routines. For a number of years, I have noted the amount of time actually devoted to Bible study in Sunday School classes, and the average time is something like thirty-five to forty minutes, except for choir members who generally excuse themselves ten minutes early to prepare for the worship service.

Statistically, about half the resident members of a church are enrolled in the Bible study program. But, on any given Sunday, only half of those enrolled are present. On the average, then, something like seventy-five percent of a church's members are not to be found in weekly Bible study.

What is even more striking is the diminished emphasis on the educational role of the pastor. The Bible provides convincing evidence that the pastors of New Testament churches were teachers. Teaching might well have been the pastor's primary ministry in many instances. The apostles were teachers. The evangelists were teachers. The Old Testament prophets, so often held up as a model for contemporary ministers, functioned basically as teachers. Yet, while it is commonplace for church people to call their pastors "preacher," seldom is a minister of the gospel called "teacher."

Except for brief readings of Scripture (still known as "lessons" in some churches), the instructional element which figured so prominently in New Testament church meetings has virtually disappeared. By and large, contemporary preaching has lost its didactic character; authentic expository preaching is all too rare.

This book grows out of a profound conviction that the New Testament church was a teaching church and that the educational function was vitally related to every other aspect of its life and ministry. I have attempted to examine the biblical backgrounds of the teaching ministry and, at the same time, to relate that heritage to the practice of Christian teaching today.

Like many other twentieth-century disciples, I am deeply concerned about the tendency of contemporary Christianity to stagnate spiritually while dancing to the tunes of a materialistic, sensate culture. I'm not sure anyone has a perfect formula for church renewal. But I am convinced of one thing: Whatever else we do to bring about the spiritual renascence that so many hope for, education must be a part of the answer. Whatever else we do, we must re-establish the priority of the ministry which Jesus placed foremost in his own work on earth, the ministry which was on the leading edge of the early Christian missionary movement, the ministry which, more than any other, sustained the vitality of infant churches in alien environments—the ministry of the taught Word.

LUCIEN E. COLEMAN, JR.
Southwestern Baptist Theological Seminary
Fort Worth, Texas

Note

1. J. Stanley Glen, *The Recovery of the Teaching Ministry* (Philadelphia: The Westminster Press, 1960), p. 9.

1
Jesus Came Teaching

Jesus of Nazareth spent his life in a tiny country just 75 miles wide and 150 miles long; but his purpose encompassed the world. He lived in relative obscurity; but he was destined to become the most influential figure in human history. He never raised an army, never staged a political revolution, never accumulated wealth, never wrote a book. Yet, he bent the trajectory of human experience more than any other individual who ever lived on this planet. The public career of Jesus lasted less than three years. But his influence has lasted for nearly 20 centuries.

How did he do it? How was he able to accomplish so much in such a short time? What was his strategy?

To answer this question, one must turn to the Gospels, the primary source documents for a study of the life of Jesus. In the Gospels the answer comes through with crystal clarity. Jesus was first and foremost a teacher.

He preached the good news of the kingdom of God; but his hearers called him Teacher. He healed the sick and comforted the troubled; but those who benefited from his ministry knew him as Teacher. He called disciples to his side; they thought of him as Teacher. He rebuked hypocrisy and sterile tradition, thus incurring the wrath of religious leaders. And even these opponents addressed him as "Teacher."

His followers would eventually come to know him as "Christ," "Savior," and "Lord." But, even beyond the resurrection, their vision of him as "Teacher" remained undiminished.

As C. H. Dodd once noted:

> It is not the least remarkable feature of the Gospels as historical documents that although they—even Mark—are written under the influence of a "high" Christology, yet they all—even John—represent Jesus as a teacher with His school of disciples.[1]

Jesus as Teacher in the Gospels

In the Gospel narratives, teaching is clearly the most characteristic activity of the ministry of Jesus.

The Greek word *didaskalos* (teacher) occurs forty-eight times in the four Gospels. In forty-two of these instances, the term refers to Jesus, usually as a form of direct address. The fact that Jesus was so frequently called Teacher is sometimes obscured by the rendering Master in the King James Version. As Lewis J. Sherrill has pointed out, "When the Bible was being translated into these earlier versions, Master (Latin: *Magister*) denoted a *schoolmaster,* but the word has now lost that meaning in ordinary speech, and some of the recent versions use the word Teacher to translate *Didaskalos.*"[2]

His disciples habitually referred to him by this title. An especially revealing illustration of this is recorded in Mark 4:35-41. Jesus and his disciples were caught in a terrifying storm while attempting to cross the Sea of Galilee in a small boat. Waves crashed over the sides of the tiny craft, threatening to take them all to the bottom. It was not a time for standing on ceremony, not an occasion for formal titles. In a situation like this, people tend to employ words which have become second nature to them. In this instance, the disciples cried out to Jesus, "Teacher (*didaskale*), do you not care if we perish?"

But this perception of Jesus as a teacher went beyond his band of followers. Nicodemus, for example, said to Jesus, "Rabbi, we know that you are a teacher [*didaskalos*] come from God" (John 3:2). The scribes and Pharisees (Matt. 8:19;12:38), disciples of the Herodians and Sadducees (Matt. 22:16,24,36) the servants of Jairus (Mark 5:35; 3:2), and unnamed persons in the crowd (Mark 9:17; Luke 9:38) all called him Teacher.

More significantly, Jesus chose the term *didaskalos* to describe himself. The Gospels record five instances in which Jesus referred to himself as Teacher (Matt. 23:8; Mark 14:14; Luke 22:11; John 1:13-14). On one of these occasions, he was sending two of his followers into Jerusalem to make arrangements for what future generations of Christians would call the Last Supper. He instructed them to say, "The Teacher says, 'Where is my guest room, where I am to eat the passover with my disciples?'" (Mark 14:14).

Teaching—His Primary Function

The verb *didaskein* (to teach) regularly describes the activity of Jesus in the Gospel narratives.

Luke tells us that Jesus inaugurated his public ministry with a teaching mission in the synagogues of Galilee

(Luke 4:14-15; cf. Matt. 4:23; 9:35; 13:54; Mark 1:21). The synagogue was an important educational institution in Jesus' day. Worship activities—prayers, petitions, and singing—were included in the weekly order of service; but the most important element of the synagogue meeting was teaching. Teaching in the synagogue was rooted in the reading of Old Testament Scriptures; specifically, the Law (Pentateuch) and the Prophets. Readings of Scripture were followed by the "discourse," a period of instruction. Luke's description of the synagogue service at Nazareth (4:16-27) clearly reflects this traditional sequence of events. What was decidedly nontraditional on this occasion was the startling content of the teaching of Jesus (4:22, 28).

The Gospels portray teaching as the integrating element in all that Jesus did during his public ministry. To be sure, his ministry included other functions. Matthew tells us, for example, that "he went about all Galilee, teaching in their synagogues, and preaching the gospel of the kingdom, and healing every disease and every infirmity among the people" (Matt. 4:23). But, still, teaching was the role which determined his identity. In none of the Gospels is Jesus called a preacher (*kerux*). As he proclaimed the good news of the kingdom, as he made broken bodies whole, those who witnessed these things called him Teacher.

When we think of his preaching, we should divest our minds of the images of pulpit oratory that are so readily conjured up by that term. Anyone who envisions Jesus delivering the Sermon on the Mount to a large congregation from a hillside rostrum simply hasn't examined Matthew's narrative (5:1-2; 7:28-29) closely. In the first place, the language strongly implies that Jesus went up into the mountain to withdraw from the crowds (5:1), although it could be argued on the basis of John 7:28-29 that he did not succeed in this. We are told, further, that Jesus "sat down," and that "his disciples came to him" (5:1). What we see at this point is not a pulpiteer standing before a congregation, but a teacher in intimate dialogue with his disciples. Finally, the text says, "he opened his mouth and taught [*edidasken*] them" (5:2). At the end of the passage, this same verb is used, along with the noun *didache,* to describe what Jesus had been doing on the mountain. "The crowds were astonished at his teaching, for he taught them as one who had authority" (7:28-29).

Are we to conclude, then, that the Sermon on the Mount is an example of teaching rather than preaching? Not at all. Actually, the passage exemplifies both the teaching and the preaching of Jesus. His preaching was defined by its content, not by a particular style of delivery. That content was the "good news of the kingdom," a subject which he would touch upon again and again in his teaching (Matt. 5:19-20; 6:13, 33; 7:21; cf. 7:13-14).

In the ministry of Jesus, teaching and preaching were twin functions. Some of the most notable teaching episodes in the Gospel accounts were direct outgrowths of his public proclamations. One such occasion is described in Matthew 13. The gathering described at the beginning of this chapter did resemble a congregation. Jesus spoke to the crowd in parables, concerning "the kingdom of heaven" (v. 11). After his public proclamation of the kingdom, Jesus used the occasion to teach his disciples the meaning of his parables in a private follow-up session (vv. 10-52).

The healing ministry of Jesus, like his preaching, was continually linked to his role as a teacher. An incident in the synagogue at Capernaum (Mark 1:21-28) illustrates this. Jesus entered the synagogue and taught with astonishing authority. Then a man with an unclean spirit challenged him. Jesus exorcised the unclean spirit, and the people expressed amazement over what they had witnessed.

What is particularly striking about this account is that the people responded to the *exorcism* by commenting on Jesus' *teaching*. "What is this?" they exclaimed, still gazing upon the man who had just been delivered of the unclean spirit. "A new teaching!" (v. 27). The act of healing had authenticated the Master's teaching.

Toward the end of his public ministry, Jesus seems to have placed increasing emphasis on teaching. In the Synoptic Gospels, he is addressed only four times as Teacher before the confession of Peter at Caesarea Philippi (Matt. 16:13-16), but twenty-two times afterward, as he turns his face toward Jerusalem where he will face certain death. As the "time of his departure" drew nearer, it became increasingly urgent that his disciples understand his mission and message. It was then that his teaching role took on added significance.

Jesus as Rabbi

"One of the most firmly fixed elements in the Synoptic tradition," wrote Burton Scott Easton, "is the fact that Jesus was regularly addressed as 'Rabbi.'"[3]

His disciples often called him Rabbi, just as they

habitually referred to him as Teacher (Matt. 26:25; Mark 9:5; 11:21; John 4:31; 9:2; 11:8). Followers of John the Baptist (John 1:38), Nicodemus (John 3:2), faceless persons in the crowds that surrounded him (John 6:25), and Judas the betrayer (Matt. 26:49) all knew Jesus as Rabbi. On two occasions, he was addressed as Rabboni, an intensified form of the title (Mark 10:51; John 20:16).

But what did this mean?

Originally an Aramaic word meaning "my great one," Rabbi was a term of respect, not unlike the English Sir, addressed to Jewish teachers of the law. In Greek texts of the New Testament, the Aramaic term is sometimes simply transliterated *rabbi.* But, in other instances, the word is translated into the Greek equivalents *didaskale* (teacher) or *epistata* (master).

These three terms—Rabbi, Teacher, Master—are used interchangeably in various English translations of the Gospels, for they all have essentially the same meaning. The author of the Fourth Gospel even makes it a point to explain that Rabbi means Teacher (John 1:38).

But a rabbi was not a *mere* teacher. Mark 1:22 draws a sharp contrast between a rabbi, one who teaches with authority, and the scribes, who had no authority of their own. The scribes were ordinary teachers who were not permitted to introduce new interpretations or render original decisions. They were the "elementary teachers" of Palestine. The villages were full of them. The rabbi, on the other hand, was endowed with unique authority conferred upon him in a special ordination ceremony by an older rabbi. In this rite of ordination, it was believed, the new rabbi received wisdom and power which was ultimately descended from Moses.[4]

Jesus taught not as the scribes, but as one who possessed rabbinic authority (Mark 1:22). But by whose hands had he been ordained? This was the question underlying the challenge of the chief priests and elders in the Temple: "By what authority are you doing these things, and who gave you this authority?" (Matt. 21:23). They were asking Jesus to name the rabbi who had conferred authority on him. Jesus did not answer their query directly; but, by raising the question about the authority of John the Baptist (21:25), he clearly meant to imply that his was a heavenly authority.

The Talmud contains evidence that Jesus might have been known to Jewish tradition as a rabbi.[5] However, it seems unlikely that the religious leaders of his day recognized him as a duly-ordained rabbi, in view of their questions concerning his credentials (Matt. 21:23). Nicodemus, a member of the Sanhedrin, did address Jesus as Rabbi on one notable occasion (John 3:1-2). But, judging from the complimentary tone of his words in verse 2, it seems logical to understand this as merely a respectful greeting, rather than as attribution of rabbinic authority in a formal sense. What is certain is that Nicodemus recognized Jesus as a teacher (*didaskalos*), and, more important, as a "teacher come from God."

Here was a religious leader who apparently was willing to be convinced that the signs performed by Jesus were evidence of a divine calling. Jesus repeatedly laid claim to such a calling (John 5:19-23, 27, 30; 7:16; 8:16). And, in so doing, he implicitly rejected the notion that he had received ordination through any human agency. He was, indeed, a teacher come from God.

It was natural for those who observed his life-style to

conclude that Jesus was a rabbi. Like a rabbi, he gathered a band of followers about him and gave them intensive instructions. He called these followers disciples (*math-etai*), employing a term which commonly denoted those who attached themselves to the person of a rabbi. To all outward appearances, his relationship to these followers was that of a rabbi to his disciples.

T. W. Manson suggested that Jesus might have deliberately drawn a contrast between his followers and the disciples of the Jewish rabbis by using an Aramaic word which meant "apprentice," rather than the more familiar *talmid* (the Hebrew equivalent of *mathetes*). Elaborating on this idea, Manson wrote:

> The *talmid* of the Rabbinical schools is primarily a student. His chief business was to master the contents of the written Law and the oral Tradition. The finished products of the Rabbinical schools were learned biblical scholars and sound and competent lawyers. The life of a *talmid* as *talmid* was made up of study of the sacred writings, attendance on lectures, and discussion of difficult passages or cases. Discipleship as Jesus conceived it was not a theoretical discipline of this sort, but a practical task to which men were called to give themselves and all their energies. Their work was not study but practice. Fishermen were to become fishers of men, peasants were to be labourers in God's vineyard or God's harvest field. And Jesus was their Master not so much as a teacher of right doctrine, but rather as the master-craftsman whom they were to follow and imitate.[6]

The disciples were, indeed, apprentices in the work of the Kingdom. As they followed the Master day by day, they learned in the laboratory of experience. They learned about prayer as Jesus communed with the Heavenly Father in quiet retreats and in public places. They grew in their understanding of self-giving service as their Master girded himself with a towel and washed their feet. Participating in teaching-healing missions under his tutelage, they enlarged their capacity for ministry. They learned about the kingdom of God as Jesus lived under the sovereignty of the Father before their very eyes. They discerned the ethics of the Kingdom as they observed firsthand the way he related to others. They learned to identify with his life-style, his values, his perceptions, and his purpose in the world. They came to understand the divine passion for all humanity as they heard their already weary Master say, "Let us go on to the next towns, that I may preach there, also; for that is why I came" (Mark 1:38).

There was yet another unique dimension in the relationship between Jesus and his disciples. Ordinarily, a rabbi and his disciple were both seekers after knowledge which lay beyond them, the essential difference between teacher and disciple being that the rabbi possessed a greater degree of this knowledge. But with Jesus it was different. Unlike other teachers, he did not stand side by side with his disciples in a search for truth. Rather, he *was* truth (John 14:6), the embodiment of the knowledge which his disciples were to seek. For them, he was both schoolmaster and subject matter. They were appointed, not to master a body of religious truth, but to "be with him" (Mark 3:14).

From the beginning, Jesus made it plain that a faith commitment would be one of the unalterable conditions of discipleship (John 14:1-6, 10-12). His was a call to radical allegiance (Matt. 10:37-39) and consistent obedience (John 14:15, 21, 23; 15:10). He was not asking for some generalized emotional response or a single reckless pledge of loyalty. (Peter tried that, you might remember; Matt. 26:33, 35.) The Teacher demanded nothing less than knowledge of and obedience to his teachings. "He that hath my commandments, and keepeth them, he it is that loveth me" (KJV), he taught his disciples (John 14:21; cf. 14:23; 15:7, 10). He made it clear that there could be no discipleship apart from obedience (John 8:31); and, of course, there could be no obedience apart from an intimate knowledge of the things which he taught.

The training of the twelve was extremely urgent. Jesus' time with them was limited. After his departure, they alone would be left to interpret his teachings to the members of the Christian community. They would be the sole link between the historical Jesus and successive generations of disciples. Therefore, they must "get it and get it right" while the Teacher was still with them.

Jesus reflects this concern in Matthew 13:51-52. The Master is with his intimate band of disciples, explaining the meaning of a parable which he has just taught in public. He asks them, "Have you understood all this?" They assure him that they have understood. Then he says, "Therefore every scribe who has been trained for the kingdom is like a householder who brings out of his treasure what is new and what is old" (Matt. v. 52).

Remember who the scribes were. They were specially trained men whose task it was to copy the written Law, to record the detailed rulings of the rabbis, and to teach these things to the people. The apostles were to have a similar task in relation to the teachings of Jesus. The Teacher intended to leave behind him a cadre of disciples who not only would remember his sayings accurately but could also be counted on to teach them to others. As subsequent New Testament history shows, that is exactly what happened. After Pentecost, the Jerusalem church continued steadfastly "[in] the apostles' teaching" (Acts 2:42; cf. 4:2; 5:42).

The importance of this historical linkage between the apostles' teaching and the teachings of Jesus himself can hardly be overemphasized. Their task, as "scribes of the kingdom," was not to teach on their own but, rather, to faithfully reproduce what had been committed to them by their Teacher.

Jesus, Teacher and Risen Lord

Teaching was the integrating function not only during the earthly ministry of the historical Jesus. It was also an important motif in his identity as the risen Lord.

In a very real sense, Jesus was the only Teacher ever recognized as such by his disciples. This was true not only during his earthly ministry but after the resurrection as well. No one would ever supersede him in this role.

"But you are not to be called rabbi," he said to his disciples on one occasion, "for you have one teacher, and you are all brethren" (Matt. 23:8). While the Jewish rabbis were greatly concerned about ordaining successors, no disciple of Jesus ever assumed that he would succeed his Master in the role of rabbi.

A dramatic encounter between the risen Christ and two of his disciples on the road to Emmaus (Luke 24:13-27) served as a reminder of the Master's continuing role as teacher. After perceiving a faintness of heart and lack of understanding in these disciples, the Teacher proceeded to instruct them. "Beginning with Moses and all the prophets, he interpreted to them in all the scriptures the things concerning himself" (v. 27).

This post-resurrection relationship between the disciples and their Master would continue a pattern which had evolved during his earthly ministry. During those early days in Galilee, he had sent them out on a training mission. Essentially, they were "practice teaching" under his supervision, going out to share with others what they had learned from him, and returning to report on "all that they had done and taught" (Mark 6:30). After the resurrection, the situation was remarkably similar. They would still be teaching under the guidance of his Spirit (John 14:26). But the "Spirit of truth," who would soon come to guide the minds of the disciples "into all the truth," was to introduce no novel teaching. His function would be to shed further light on the teachings of Jesus (John 16:13-15). The risen Lord would still be *the* Teacher.

In the opening words of Acts, Luke indirectly attests to the early church's belief in the continuing teaching activity of the risen Lord. With reference to his earlier treatise (Luke's Gospel), he writes, "The former treatise have I made, O Theophilus, of all that Jesus *began* [italics mine] both to do and to teach" (v. 1, KJV). What had been described in the Gospel of Luke was only a beginning. Luke's historical narrative in Acts would continue the story of the risen Lord working with and teaching his people. And, for all who acknowledge his lordship, the story continues even to this day.

Notes

1. C. H. Dodd, "Jesus as Teacher and Prophet," G. K. A. Bell and Adolf Deissmann, eds., *Mysterium Christi* (London: Longmans, Green and Co., 1930), p. 53.
2. Lewis J. Sherrill, *The Rise of Christian Education* (New York: The Macmillan Co., 1944), p. 85*f.*
3. Burton Scott Easton, "The First Evangelic Tradition," *Journal of Biblical Literature,* 50 (1931), p. 148.
4. David Daube, *The New Testament and Rabbinic Judaism* (London: University of London, The Athlone Press, 1956), pp. 206-7.
5. Dodd, p. 53.
6. T. W. Manson, *The Teaching of Jesus* (Cambridge: Cambridge University Press, 1963), pp. 239-40.

2
The Teaching Church

The early pages of the Book of Acts bring to mind the stirring events of Pentecost—the sound of a rushing wind, tongues as of fire, Spirit-inspired witnessing, the bold preaching of Peter, and an extraordinary ingathering of converts. What is less obvious to the casual reader is that teaching was as close to the heartbeat of that early Christian community as were prayer and preaching. Teaching was a vital function from which the young church drew spiritual life.

"Go . . . Teaching"

Those early Christians taught because Jesus had made teaching a priority strategy in his own ministry. What a strange paradox it would have been for the disciples of the Master Teacher to have neglected the task of teaching.

But, more important, Jesus had specifically commanded his followers to teach in the "Great Commission" (Matt. 28:19-20), his marching orders to the church for all generations. The Revised Standard Version's "Go therefore and make disciples of all nations" (v. 19) is a more accurate translation than the King James Version's "teach all nations." The Greek verb used here is *matheteusate,* which means "to disciple." As applied to Christian discipleship, the term embraces the concepts of repentance, radical conversion, and submission to the lordship of Jesus Christ. But it also implies lifelong enrollment in the school of Christian learning, for the essence of discipleship is learnership. A disciple who disdains learning is no less paradoxical than a cowboy who won't go near horses.

The Christian disciple, however, is not a learner who examines random bits of information in the hope that they might prove more or less useful someday. A disciple of the Lord Jesus Christ is a person who is willing to have his life changed by what he learns from his Master. "To disciple," in the context of the Great Commission, means to lead individuals to acknowledge the lordship of Jesus Christ in repentance and faith and to submit themselves to a continuing process of instruction which will radically alter their lives.

There can be no doubt about the meaning of the participial phrase, "teaching [*didaskontes*] them to observe all that I have commanded you" (Matt. 28:20). Jesus clearly intended for his disciples to instruct converts in all his teachings just as he had instructed his first disciples during his earthly ministry. To lead men and women to call Jesus "Lord" without knowing and doing the things he taught would have been an unthinkable distortion of his purpose (Luke 6:46).

Unfortunately, such a distortion of the Great Commission is not so unthinkable today. Modern Christianity is seriously infected by a truncated form of evangelism which cares little for the teaching of disciples, before or after baptism. This is more than a mildly regrettable oversight. It is spiritual arrogance; for it repudiates the explicit command of Jesus himself. The very syntax of the Great Commission makes it clear that teaching is not optional. This passage contains three participles—going, baptizing, teaching—all equal in rank grammatically, all equal in importance operationally. To concentrate exclusively on "going" and "baptizing" without regard for "teaching" is to ignore part of the Lord's command.

The Apostles' Teaching

Luke's narrative in Acts 2:41-42 leaves no doubt that the earliest Christians acted on the Great Commission in its entirety. This account reports that the unusual events of Pentecost resulted in about 3,000 conversions. Then, immediately after their baptism, we find that these new believers "devoted themselves to the apostles' teaching [*didache*]" (v. 42).

Teaching was a mainline strategy in the evangelistic activity of those early apostles. They went into the Temple area and "taught the people, and preached through Jesus the resurrection from the dead" (Acts 4:2, KJV). The religious authorities, disturbed by the effectiveness of these Christian witnesses, tried to put a stop to the activities that were doing the most damage. They warned the apostles "not to speak or teach at all in the name of Jesus" (4:18; also see 5:28). Yet, heeding the mandate of the risen Lord, the apostles pursued their mission. "Every day in the temple and at home they did not cease teaching and preaching Jesus as the Christ" (5:42).

In these passages, the functions of teaching and preaching flow into one another. Luke evidently regarded these as distinct activities, since he repeatedly used both terms. But what were the distinguishing characteristics of each?

C. H. Dodd attempted to draw a sharp line between the preaching (*kerygma*) and the teaching (*didache*) of the apostles, partially on the basis of the content of the message. He concluded that the apostolic preaching was the public proclamation of Christ to the non-Christian world, while the teaching of the apostles was primarily ethical instruction directed to the Christian community.[1] There is a measure of truth in this view, but Dodd drew the line too firmly, for, in the passages cited earlier (Acts 4:2; 4:18; 5:28, 42), the apostles were said to be teaching even in contexts where they were proclaiming Christ publicly to non-Christian audiences. Dodd himself acknowledged that the apostles' teaching occasionally "seems to include what we should call apologetic, that is, the reasoned commendation of Christianity to persons interested, but not yet convinced."[2]

The teaching of the apostles was often *kerygmatic,* marked by proclamation of the gospel. And their preaching was often *didactic,* obviously instructional in nature. The sermons in Acts typically contain expositions of Old Testament Scriptures, similar to those heard weekly in the synagogues. In truth, the gospel was frequently presented in the synagogues, undoubtedly during the part of the service set aside for instruction (Acts 13:14-42; 14:1; 17:1-4, 17; 18:4, 26).

Were these presentations of the Christian message thought of as "preaching" or "teaching"? The question probably would not have occurred to first-century Christians. The language in Acts is inconclusive, for Luke uses a variety of terms to describe the communication activity of Christian witnesses among the Jews. The message was sometimes proclaimed (9:20), sometimes delivered in the form of a polemic lecture (17:20), sometimes taught (28:31). But, in most instances, the message was delivered in an instructional setting. And, whether "taught" or "preached," it was designed to win converts.

Peter's sermon delivered in Solomon's porch (3:11-26) illustrates the close correlation between the apostolic proclamation of the gospel and the apostolic teaching of the ethical demands of the Christian way. In this passage the proclamation (*kerygma*) of Christ is couched in the form of a narrative, laced with Old Testament prophecy and combined with a call to repentance (vv. 13-26). In verse 22, Peter presents Jesus as the Second Moses who must be heard "in whatever he tells you." The teachings of this Second Moses must be taken just as seriously and obeyed just as diligently as the Israelites were to have heard and obeyed the Law delivered through the first Moses.

How might the people know the message of this Second Moses, that they might obey? This question found its answer in the teaching of the apostles. They had been commissioned by Jesus himself to communicate his moral teachings to the next generation of Christians. The "whatever he tells you" in Acts 3:22 is equivalent to the "all that I have commanded you" in Matthew 28:20.

The Diffusion of the Teaching Function

At first, the apostles themselves were the teachers of the Christian community. It was only natural that they should perform this function since they had been with the Master. They could truly say, "That which we have seen and heard we proclaim also to you" (1 John 1:3). But it was inevitable that the ministry of teaching would soon be shared with others, for the apostles would eventually face enormous logistical challenges.

Easton described what he called a "pedagogical problem without parallel" within the burgeoning Jerusalem congregation following Pentecost.[3] In a short while, the Christian community grew dramatically (Acts 2:41; 4:4), and so did the teaching task. Under the best of circumstances, it would have strained the energies of the twelve to maintain a continuing program of instruction for so many converts. But there were further complications. These first Christian converts, Easton pointed out, "came chiefly from the lower classes, and were in large measure what the Jews called 'sinners'; persons long indifferent to the practices of religion and unaccustomed since their school days to learning religious rules."[4] To make matters worse, most of these persons were in poverty and, undoubtedly, found it necessary to devote long hours each day to eking out a bare existence. They would have had little time for learning.

Remember, too, that the teacher was the learner's sole source of information. There was no printed material, no textbooks, no lesson periodicals to be utilized in individual study. The sayings of Jesus, at this time, had to be learned by rote as they came from the mouths of the apostles.

Finally, we must take into account the fact that teaching was not the only responsibility of the apostles. They were also evangelists, worship leaders, and administrators of the affairs of the congregation. Given such a ponderous work load, they soon asked the congregation to choose seven men of good report to help with administrative and pastoral tasks (Acts 6:3).

The circumstances just described would seem to point inescapably to the conclusion that other members of the congregation took up the task of teaching along with the apostles. The narrative at this point in Acts contains no explicit evidence that others were officially ordained as teachers; but we do know that other believers began to function as teachers.

Philip, for example, one of the "seven," became an effective minister of the Word. On the basis of the terminology alone, one would have to conclude that he functioned as a preacher and an evangelist (Acts 8:5, 12, 35, 40). But the account of his interview with the Ethiopian eunuch (8:27-35) pictures him as a teaching evangelist. The Ethiopian expressed a desire to have someone "guide" him, as he attempted to read the Scriptures. So Philip seated himself beside the man and, in this one-on-one situation, helped him understand how the prophecy of Isaiah related to Jesus Christ. The terminology used in verse 35 tells us that Philip "began at the same scripture, and preached unto him Jesus." (The verb preached here translates the Greek *euaggelisato,* which more literally means something like "announced the good news.") What happened in that chariot was an intimate dialogue between a Spirit-led teacher and an eager learner.

The geographical dispersion of Christianity created an ever-widening circle of teachers in the churches. In Acts 13, where the scene shifts suddenly to Antioch in Syria, we find prophets and teachers at work in that congregation. Saul of Tarsus was among these spiritual leaders. The grammatical structure of this verse in the Greek text suggests that Luke intended to classify Saul, along with Manaen, as a teacher, in contradistinction to the prophets —Barnabas, Simeon, and Lucius. Saul was soon to embark on an overseas missionary career (13:2-3). He and Barnabas would carry the gospel across new frontiers (15:36). Later descriptions of this spiritual odyssey make it clear that teaching was a major missionary strategy.

Soon a bright new teacher of the Scriptures, a "Jew named Apollos," appeared on the scene at Ephesus (Acts 18:24-25). At this point in his career, he was in need of further instruction in the faith; for his knowledge of Christian tradition was limited. So, "Priscilla and Aquila . . . took him and expounded to him the way of God more accurately" (v. 26).

Wherever the gospel took root, wherever Christian communities grew up, there Christian teachers were found. The writings of Paul contain ample evidence of this. To the Corinthians he wrote, "God has appointed in the church first apostles, second prophets, third teachers [*didaskaloi*]" (1 Cor. 12:28). Again, in Romans, teaching appears among the first three functions mentioned by Paul in a discussion of spiritual gifts in the church: "If our gift is to speak God's message, we should do it according to the faith that we have; if it is to serve, we should serve; if it is to teach, we should teach" (Rom. 12:6-7, GNB). Galatians 6:6, also makes it clear that there were persons within the congregation who were designated as teachers.

The Pastoral Epistles, representing a later period of development, abound with references to teaching. Fifteen of the twenty-one occurrences of the word *didaskalia*, "teaching," in the New Testament appear in the

Pastorals. In these letters, Timothy and Titus (both presumably pastors) are repeatedly urged to give attention to teaching (1 Tim. 4:6, 11, 13, 16; 6:2; 2 Tim. 2:2, 24; 4:2; Titus 2:2, 7). Bishops must be skilled at teaching (1 Tim. 3:2; Titus 1:9). Elders who labor at preaching and teaching are to be considered "worthy of double honor" (1 Tim. 5:17). Older women (an official group, perhaps) are to "teach what is good" (Titus 2:3).

Looking at the New Testament evidence as a whole, it seems reasonable to draw two conclusions: first, that the responsibility for teaching was delegated to a variety of elected church leaders; second, that the privilege of teaching was by no means confined to official leaders. In fact, Colossians 3:16 indicates that the teaching function was mutually shared by all the members of the gathered congregation.

In some passages where the word *teacher* occurs, it probably is best to understand the term as a function rather than as an official title. In Acts 13:1, for example, Luke calls Saul a teacher but later refers to him by the more technical title, "apostle" (Acts 14:14). Paul himself seems to have preferred the designation "apostle" (Rom. 1:1, 5; 1 Cor. 1:1; 9:1-2; 15:9; Gal. 1:1). Yet, he remained in Corinth for a year and a half "teaching the word of God" (Acts 18:11).

Barnabas, on the other hand, was numbered among the prophets at Antioch (Acts 13:1), but functioned as both teacher and preacher in his missionary work (15:-35).

Ephesians 4:11 makes it clear that the teaching function was embedded in the pastor's role. "And his gifts were that some should be apostles, some prophets, some evangelists, some pastors and teachers," the passage reads. In the Greek text, the construction of the phrase, "pastors and teachers," with one definite article indicates that these two functions were lodged in the same individuals. Pastors were expected to play an active role in the educational function of the church. Teaching was not a duty to be added to the work of the pastor when no one else could be recruited to do it. Teaching was a part of the pastor's responsibility, no less than preaching.

The teaching which had begun with Jesus during his earthly ministry was passed on to the twelve, who in turn became the first teachers in the Jerusalem congregation. Very soon, though, many other church leaders were functioning as teachers. These included evangelists, pastors, prophets, bishops, elders, and deacons. In addition, there were a good many persons within Christian congregations who held no formal offices, but who functioned as teachers.

Why did teaching become so widely distributed among the leaders and members of New Testament congregations? It seems that there was a great deal of teaching to be done. Teaching was not optional. It belonged to the very heartbeat of these young Christian communities of faith. No congregation could afford to neglect teaching. And no believer was exempt from responsibility for learning to observe all that Jesus had commanded.

What the Church Taught

Lewis J. Sherrill has identified five kinds of teaching which appeared in the early Christian churches within the lifetime of the apostles. These were: (1) the Christian interpretation of Old Testament Scriptures; (2) the teaching of the gospel; (3) the Christian's confession of his faith; (4) the life and sayings of Jesus; and (5) the Christian way of life.[5]

The New Testament is replete with examples of the first kind of teaching, Christian interpretations of Old Testament Scriptures. Jesus himself continually referred to the Old Testament in his teaching (for example, Matt. 5:21, 27, 31, 33, 38, 43; 12:17-21; 13:14-15; Luke 4:17-19; 6:3-4; 10:26f.; 20:17, 42-43).

The discourses of the early evangelists recorded in the Book of Acts invariably contained expositions of Old Testament Scriptures (see Acts 2:17-21, 25-28, 34-35; 3:22; 7:2-50; 8:30f.; 13:16-41, 47; 15:15-18; 28:26-27). In one of the closing scenes in Acts we find Paul, now under house arrest in Rome, speaking to a gathering of Jewish brethren, "trying to convince them about Jesus both from the law of Moses and from the prophets" (28:23).

The Book of Hebrews contains numerous quotations of Old Testament Scriptures and references to Old Testament history. These include, for example, the discourse on the uniqueness of Christ's priesthood based on references to the priesthood of Melchizedek (Heb. 5:5-10; 7:1-17), and the well-known "roll call of the faithful" in Hebrews 11.

We cannot fully appreciate the importance of this element in early Christian teaching unless we take into account the significant role which the synagogue played in the shaping of Christian worship and teaching.

Jesus frequently taught in the synagogues; and his disciples followed this pattern. First-generation Christians did not look upon the gospel of Jesus Christ as a repudiation of their Jewish heritage but rather as a fulfillment of it. This was the attitude of Jesus himself (Matt. 5:17). It was only natural, therefore, for those early Christians to continue going to their synagogues in order to interpret the Scriptures in light of their experience in Christ.

It was in the synagogues of Damascus that the newly-converted Saul of Tarsus first bore witness to his faith in Jesus Christ (Acts 9:20). Ironically, these were the very synagogues whose help he had previously sought in his persecution of the followers of Christ.

Again and again the synagogues provided a point of contact in the cities visited by Christian missionaries as they penetrated the Mediterranean world (Acts 13:5, 14f., 42-43; 14:1; 17:1-2, 17; 18:4, 7, 26). The invariable practice of the synagogue was to base the weekly instructional discourse upon a reading of the Scriptures. Thus, what is said of Philip's interview with the Ethiopian eunuch, "and beginning with this scripture he told him the good news of Jesus" (Acts 8:35), could be said of every Christian who taught in a synagogue.

Christian interpretations of Old Testament Scriptures were not always received in passive docility by Jewish hearers (Acts 18:4-7; 19:8-9; 28:23-27). In the crucible of competing ideas, as Christian witnesses were compelled to develop arguments and counterarguments against Jewish detractors, this form of Christian teaching became more and more refined. Some interpreters believe that portions of the New Testament grew out of this developing tradition. Krister Stendahl has argued convincingly that the Gospel of Matthew came out of a school for training early church leaders, a school "with its ingenious interpretation of the Old Testament as the crown of its scholarship."[6]

The gospel message was another significant element in the curriculum of the primitive church. Paul underscored the importance of the gospel when he wrote to the Romans, "For I am not [disappointed] in the gospel: it is the power of God for salvation to everyone who has faith" (Rom. 1:16).

Today there are those who think that anything spoken from the pulpit is "gospel." But Paul and his contemporaries had something quite specific in mind when they used the term. In 1 Corinthians 15:3-5, we find a succinct outline of the elements of the gospel, focusing on the meaning of Christ's death in light of the Scriptures, his burial, and his resurrection as attested to by post-resurrection appearances.

The gospel was at the heart of the apostolic preaching. Paul did not speak directly of "teaching" the gospel, nor did he use the characteristic word for "preaching." Rather, he used the verb *euaggelizomai* in reference to his communication of the gospel. This term is difficult to render in English, since it is a cognate form of *euaggelion,* the word which means *gospel.* Thus, if we take the verb *euaggelizomai* quite literally, we must translate it something like "gospelling the gospel." Since this would be redundant, translators prefer to render the term "preach" or "announce," or simply transliterate it "evangelize." The point of this, in our present discussion, is that Paul's references to "proclaiming the gospel" do not necessarily refer to utterances from a pulpit, nor does the terminology preclude what contemporary Christians would recognize as teaching.

The gospel had a significant place in the subject matter taught by Paul and his contemporaries. Paul's concern for keeping the gospel free of distortion is an urgent theme in Galatians. In this letter he tells his readers about his resistance to Judaizers, in order that the "truth of the gospel" might *continue* with them (2:5). The gospel needed to be continually communicated not only to outsiders but also to those who were within the household of faith, in order that they might understand it fully, articulate it clearly, and share it with fidelity.

In his correspondence with the Christians at Corinth, Paul reminded them that he was their "father in Christ Jesus through the gospel" (1 Cor. 4:15). It was he who had first introduced them to the gospel. And Luke's account of the apostle's initial ministry in the city of Corinth leaves no doubt that he had accomplished this primarily through teaching. Luke wrote (Acts 18:11), "And he stayed [literally, 'he sat'] a year and six months, teaching the word of God among them." He had "fathered" the Corinthian church by teaching them the gospel.

A third kind of teaching in the early church had to do with the individual's confession of faith. All Christian instruction during the New Testament period was anchored in personal faith and commitment. It began not with a collection of wisdom sayings and ethical guidelines, as in the sayings of Confucius, but with a Person. The disciple was called upon not to learn *about* Christ, but to learn Christ (Eph. 4:20). Therefore, the individual's confession of faith in Jesus as Christ and Lord was of pivotal importance.

Paul underscored the centrality of the Christian's

confession of faith in Romans 10:9-10; and, in so doing, he also offered his readers an important clue concerning the content of that confession: "If you confess with your lips that Jesus is Lord and believe in your heart that God raised him from the dead, you will be saved."

Predating even the Gospels (see 1 Cor. 12:3), the formula *Kurios Iesous* was the prototypal confession in that early community of faith (cf. Phil. 2:11; Acts 2:36). Simple in form, this confession was powerful in its import.

In the Septuagint (the Greek version of the Old Testament and Apocrypha known in Jesus' day), *Kurios* (Lord) was used to translate two names for God, *Adonai* and *Yahweh*. Thus, to call Jesus "Lord" was from the perspective of Hebrew tradition to acknowledge his power over the world and all who dwell within it, and to ascribe to Jesus the status of Creator, Ruler, and giver of life and death.

The term *lord* was also widely used in the ancient Eastern world to denote pagan deities. The Egyptians applied the title to the gods Osiris, Serapis, and Isis, and to the ruler Ptolemy XIII who, in a first-century BC inscription, was lauded as "lord, king, God." The Greeks called the goddess Artemis of Ephesus *kurios*. And, in the Roman world, the emperors Caligula, Claudius, Nero, and Domitian were often addressed as "lord."

For a Christian to confess "Jesus is Lord" was to acknowledge Jesus' absolute sovereignty over one's personal life, over the moral and spiritual realm, and, indeed, over the whole cosmic order (Col. 1:16-18). Such a confession was not to be taken lightly. To the Romans, it was potentially treasonous. To many of the Jews, it was blasphemous. To Christians, it was absolutely essential to saving faith. The early church made sure that converts knew the full meaning of what they were confessing before and after baptism.

If personal confession of faith in Jesus Christ were the foundation of the church's curriculum, the teachings of Jesus and descriptions of his life and ministry, handed down by faithful witnesses, were the building blocks of faithful discipleship. This constituted a fourth area of Christian instruction in the early church. The teachings of Jesus were regarded within the Christian community as commands, absolutely obligatory upon those who called him Lord (Luke 6:46). His were the words of eternal life (John 6:68), the revelation of the Father's will (John 16:15). The disciple who did not keep the commandments of Jesus did not love him (John 14:21, 23-24) and, in fact, was not truly a disciple (John 8:31).

It would never have occurred to those first Christians to separate faith in Jesus as Savior from obedience to him as Lord. The Master had called them to trust *and* obey. This made it a matter of crucial importance to instruct each generation of disciples in the sayings of Jesus; for one cannot obey what one does not know.

It was equally important for the church to teach the story of Jesus' life and ministry; for the words of the Master were inseparable from the events of his life. The story of the healing of a man with an unclean spirit (Mark 1:21-28), for example, demonstrated the authority of Jesus as a teacher come from God. The teachings of Jesus were repeatedly authenticated by the signs which he performed, as reported in the Fourth Gospel. The feeding of the multitude provided a dramatic background for his revelation of himself as the "bread of life" (John 6). The

raising of Lazarus undergirded his claim, "I am the resurrection and the life" (John 11:25).

Paul's Corinthian correspondence contains two excel-
lent examples of the narrative material which was communicated through the teaching ministry of the early
church. The tradition concerning the institution of the
Lord's Supper recorded in 1 Corinthians 11:23f. had
previously been shared with the congregation at Corinth
(v. 23), presumably during Paul's extended teaching
ministry there (Acts 18:1-11). Again, in 1 Corinthians
15:1-8, the apostle referred to a tradition which he had
received from others (v. 3), probably not long after his
conversion.

Hosts of unnamed men and women in the scattered
Christian communities must have patiently worked at the
task of collecting, preserving, and sharing the materials
which would eventually be incorporated into the Gospels
as we know them, the accounts of what Jesus had said and
done. Luke pays tribute to these unnamed witnesses at
the beginning of his Gospel:

> Inasmuch as many have undertaken to compile a narrative
> of the things which have been accomplished among us,
> just as they were delivered to us by those who from the
> beginning were eyewitnesses and ministers of the word,
> it seemed good to me also, having followed all things
> closely for some time past, to write an orderly account for
> you (Luke 1:1-3).

It seems highly probable that those "ministers of the
word" spoken of by Luke included Christian teachers
who, without benefit of printed materials, faithfully con-

veyed the story of Jesus to subsequent generations of believers.

The fifth kind of teaching in the early church had to do with the Christian way of life. It was inevitable that the church would soon develop a body of instructional materials related to Christian conduct. The gospel which had begun with the simple declaration, "That which we have seen and heard we proclaim also to you" (1 John 1:3), soon pushed out into the lands surrounding the Mediterranean Sea, crossing new cultural, social, and political frontiers.

Questions began to proliferate: What does Christianity mean in relation to slavery? What should be the attitude of men toward women, aristocrats toward social outcasts, Jews toward Gentiles? Should apostles earn their bread by working with their hands, or should they be supported by the congregations among whom they labored? Should believers marry unbelievers, or stay married to unbelievers after conversion? Was remarriage permissible in light of the teachings of Jesus? Were Christians entirely free from the law in the arena of everyday behavior? How should citizens of heaven conduct themselves as subjects of earthly rulers?

These and many other questions had to be answered, then taught to followers of the Way. Teaching of this kind was a dynamic process, never static. As new situations developed, the instructional task of the church became ever more complex. It was not sufficient simply to repeat the sayings of Jesus and the teachings of the apostles. These teachings now had to be reinterpreted in the light of new and unique circumstances. For example, should a Christian go on buying good, inexpensive cuts of meat that came from carcasses left over from pagan sacrifices? Had not Jesus said, "Whatever goes into a man from outside cannot defile him, since it enters not his heart but his stomach" (Mark 7:18-19)? But what if a Christian were to eat such meat while convinced in his heart that he was doing wrong? Would that be sin?

Such questions called for teachers of unusual sensitivity and insight—Spirit-filled teachers, not mere guardians of yesterday's rules. James Dunn has concluded that teachers had a twofold function in Pauline communities. First, they were responsible for passing on the tradition which had been received originally from the apostles. But, second, they were interpreters of tradition and, consequently, developers of it. The first task required a good memory. The second depended upon the inspiration of the Spirit. "As a teacher moved beyond the simple passing on of tradition to its interpretation," said Dunn, "so the locus of his authority moved more from tradition to charisma."[7]

As Dunn implied, instruction in the Christian way of life was a vital, creative enterprise, not a static recitation of regulations fixed in concrete. New Testament writers consistently urged Christian conduct, not as a formula for becoming good but as a response to God's grace in the experience of the believer.

Paul urged the Thessalonians to "lead a life worthy of God, who calls you into his own kingdom and glory" (1 Thess. 2:12). The verb "lead" is a translation of *peripatein,* which literally means "walk around" or "go about." The point is worth making, because this word virtually became a technical term for living the Christian life. Paul used the word to refer to "all who walk by this rule"

(Gal. 6:16), and to urge Christians to "lead a life worthy of the Lord" (Col. 1:10; literally, "walk worthy of the Lord"). And in Romans 6:4, "We are buried therefore with him by baptism into death, so that as Christ was raised from the dead by the glory of the Father, we too might walk in newness of life."

Notes

1. C. H. Dodd, *The Apostolic Preaching and Its Developments* (London: Hodder & Stoughton Ltd., 1944), pp. 7-8.
2. Ibid.
3. Burton Scott Easton, "The First Evangelic Tradition," *Journal of Biblical Literature,* 50 (1931), p. 151*f.*
4. Ibid.
5. Lewis J. Sherrill, *The Rise of Christian Education* (New York: The Macmillan Co., 1944), pp. 144-51.
6. Krister Stendahl, *The School of St. Matthew and Its Use of the Old Testament* (Lund: C. W. K. Gleerup, 1954), p. 34.
7. James D. G. Dunn, *Jesus and the Spirit* (London: SCM Press Ltd., 1975), pp. 282-84.

3
A Different Kind of Teaching

In his monograph *Education in the New Testament,* Ian A. Muirhead inquired: "If we accept it that religious education is a necessary and indeed inevitable preoccupation of the Christian church, what, if anything, can be said about its essential nature?"

Elaborating on his question, Muirhead went on to ask:

> Are we to regard it as a hybrid, composed of education —itself a purely secular technique—and of Christianity, drawn from another source, rather artificially put together to serve certain demands made sociologically on the Church? Do we look upon it as the application of a certain kind of know-how to the practical needs of the Christian community? Or can we say something different about it.?[1]

Muirhead's questions focused on the very issue to which this chapter is addressed. Is Christian teaching merely the practice of educational technology in a God key? Is it nothing more than the treatment of religious subject matter in basically the same way English literature and social studies are handled? Or is it different? If so, in what way is it different from other education?

Floyd Filson effectively drew the line between Christian teaching and other kinds of teaching when he wrote:

> We may think of a teacher as an instructor in a technical skill, or in some cultural or business interest, or in an academic atmosphere as a transmitter of information, a guide, or a trainer. These conceptions are totally foreign to the biblical ideal for the teacher. In the biblical view, the teacher is called of God to aid men in understanding the meaning of life in a God-centered world, and to guide them in finding, facing, and fulfilling the divine will.[2]

But this raises an equally significant question. Is Christian teaching so different that it discourages all comparison with other kinds of teaching? The question is important, because an affirmative answer would rule out any further discussion of such things as instructional objectives, methodology, and principles of curriculum design in the practice of Christian education. And this would negate the conviction held by many religious educators that Christian teachers have a great deal to learn from the accumulated experience of instructional theorists and educational practitioners.

Learning does, in fact, take place best under certain conditions; and wise teachers try to discover those conditions and teach in accordance with them. Christian teachers are not exempt from the psychological and social dynamics which influence the teaching-learning process. It is just as bad for a church teacher to create cognitive confusion by unleashing disorganized presentations upon students as it is for a history teacher to do the same. An insensitive Christian leader who cares little about the motivational state of learners can kill the desire to learn just as readily as any other teacher. Instructional content must be suited to the level of learners, whether in a Sunday School class or a humanities course.

What, then, is the relationship between Christian teaching and any other kind of teaching? The purpose of this chapter is to highlight certain distinctive elements in Christian teaching, then to present observations about its relationship to educational theory in general.

Christian Teaching Is Distinctive in Purpose

On a cold, rain-soaked night in Oxford, England, I went to hear a lecture on the subject, "The Objectives of Religious Education." In Great Britain, of course, religious education has to do with the teaching of religious subject matter in state-supported schools. The lecturer suggested that teachers of religion should help students attain knowledge and develop healthy attitudes; but he was careful to stress the point that religious education courses should not be taught so as to seek commitment from students. This, he felt, would be inappropriate in a school system supported by the public treasury of a pluralistic society.

As he spoke, I became acutely aware of the basic difference between Christian teaching and the teaching of religion. Religion might be studied, examined, pondered, and dissected in impassive detachment; but authentic Christian teaching can never be divorced from a call to commitment. It requires commitment on the part of the teacher and seeks commitment from the learner.

To divorce Christian teaching from the concept of personal commitment is to deny its essential nature; for the ultimate purpose of Christian teaching is to lead individuals into a right relationship with God through faith in Jesus Christ as Savior and obedience to his will as Lord. The Christian teacher embraces the declaration of purpose voiced by the writer of the Fourth Gospel, "that ye might believe that Jesus is the Christ, the Son of God; and that believing ye might have life through his name" (John 20:31, KJV).

Christian teaching involves the giving and receiving of information, but acquisition of information is not regarded as an end in itself. It is the means by which individuals are led to live in full accord with the will of God. Christian knowledge, which is both the content and the product of Christian teaching, is existential and personal, rather than speculative and abstract. It intercepts the learner at the core of his being, providing insight and demanding response. It addresses itself to the whole person, not to the head alone.

This is not to say that Christian knowledge is devoid of intellectual content. In 1 Corinthians 14:6-19, Paul characterizes knowledge, prophecy, and teaching as rational communication, and he specifically contrasts this with non-rational glossolalia (speaking in a tongue). The Bible offers no support for the notion that cerebral activity is unrelated to spiritual illumination. Words, concepts, metaphors, doctrinal formulations, and historical data are the solid substance of the Christian teaching-learning transaction. But the teaching of the Word is not merely the dissemination of words; it is a process in which teacher and learner alike are called to repentance, faith, and submission to the sovereignty of God.

Christian Teaching Is Centered in a Unique Person

Mark's Gospel tells us that Jesus "appointed twelve to be with him" (3:14). Later, he would send them out on a teaching-preaching-healing mission; but, first, they must *be with him*. In his school for disciples, he was both teacher and subject matter. Jesus not only spoke the word of God; he *was* the Word of God. In him were the words of eternal life (John 6:68). His teaching was a direct expression of the mind of the Father (John 7:16). To those who followed him, he was the way, the truth, and the life (John 14:6). He was not a teacher participating with his pupils in a mutual quest for truth. He was the Teacher, the source of all truth.

His words were carefully passed on to subsequent generations of believers long after the resurrection. The church confessed him as Lord. They expected to be judged by their response to what he had taught and done; therefore, it was a matter of paramount importance for them to remember what he had said and done. They were under obligation to regard his teaching as uncompromisingly binding.

In connection with this, Burton Scott Easton wrote:

> . . . on Christian lips the exhortation "Repent!" meant "Repent of your conduct as judged by Jesus' standard!" So a convert admitted merely because he accepted Jesus' Messiahship would be regarded by the Christians as still most immature. To call Jesus "Lord" and not do the things that he said was wholly unprofitable; if a convert did not know what Jesus had said, he must learn this at once.[3]

Today, no less than in the first century, Christian teaching is centered in the person of Jesus Christ. This means not only that his teachings constitute an important part of the curriculum but also that the Teacher is present whenever teachers and learners come together in his name (Matt. 18:20). Christians acknowledge the demand of John 14:15, "If you love me, you will keep my commandments," as well as the promise of verse 26, "But the Counselor, the Holy Spirit, whom the Father will send in my name, he will teach you all things, and bring to your remembrance all that I have said to you." Keeping his commandments—and, therefore, knowing them—is obligatory upon those who call him Lord. But his Spirit illuminates the way as his people seek to understand his commandments and their implications in the twentieth-century world.

Were it not for this intervention of the Spirit, Christian teaching and learning would fall prey to a new legalism not unlike that of the scribes and Pharisees during Jesus' public ministry. Keeping his commandments is not a matter of slavish conformity to ready-made laws or endless lists of regulations. As societies change and technological innovations appear, as the customs and folkways of today evolve into the historical curiosities of tomorrow, Christians must redefine their moral responsibilities again and again.

How do you live out a gospel, which originated on an ancient Galilean hillside, in the steel and polymer towers of Houston? Such questions continually demand clarification. And followers of Christ must continually rely upon the Spirit of Truth to help them discern the way.

Christian Teaching is Rooted in a Unique Word

The Bible is the textbook of the Christian faith. It always has been. From the beginning, interpretation and clarification of the Scriptures has played a prominent role in the work of Christian teachers. Jesus repeatedly referred to Old Testament passages. The early pages of Acts make it clear that his disciples carried on in this tradition. The Pauline Epistles are replete with references to the Old Testament Scriptures (Rom. 1:2; 4:3; 9:17; 10:11; 15:4; 16:26; 1 Cor. 15:3-4; Gal. 3:8,22; 4:30), and we may logically conclude that interpretations of Scripture figured prominently in his face-to-face teaching ministry as well.

Scripture-centered teaching was of fundamental importance in the churches of the New Testament period. Obviously, it was imperative for believers from a Jewish background to understand the Christian significance of Old Testament passages. So much of the church's understanding of Jesus rested on this foundation. But it was equally important for Gentile converts to be instructed in the Scriptures so they might be equipped to cope with the assaults of Judaizing and pagan influences.

In time, the oral tradition of the church became solidified. The sayings of Jesus, which at first had been reported by the apostles, were eventually circulated in written form; and, along with these, the correspondence which we know as the New Testament Epistles. As the New Testament canon developed, "according to the Scriptures" took on broader meaning.

The Christian attitude toward the Scriptures was roughly analogous to the Jewish regard for the Law as an educative force. During the Old Testament period, the only true educator of Israel was God himself; and the Law was the supreme revelation of the mind of God. The ultimate purpose of education was to live in conformity with the divine will, and that purpose could be achieved only through knowledge of the Law. This concept of the Law as a powerful agent of education comes through clearly in Psalm 119 (see especially vv. 9, 11, 24, 27, 29, 32, 36-37, 44-45, 59-61, 66, 104-105). In similar fashion, New Testament Christians attached great importance to the Scriptures as a vehicle for teaching, reproof, correction, and instruction in righteousness (2 Tim. 3:16).

This concept found an articulate spokesman in Gregory of Nyssa in the fourth century. To him, the essence of Christian education was the formation of the believer according to the image of Christ. And diligent Bible study was the means of attaining this goal. Gregory repeatedly associated the Greek verb *paideuein,* which represented one of the great classical concepts of education, with scriptural citations. Instead of using the more familiar formula, "the prophet Isaiah says," or "the apostle says," Gregory typically wrote, "the prophet Isaiah educates (*paideuei*) us" or "the apostle educates us."[4]

The Bible continued to occupy this central place in the education of Christians because its authors had been inspired by the Spirit, the divine agent of education who has always been at work in the world.

The Bible is still central to Christian teaching. It is an indispensable sourcebook for the making of disciples because it comprises the primary documents of the Christian faith. Without the Bible, we would know virtually nothing about the life and teachings of Jesus. We could not keep his commandments because we would have no knowledge of his commandments. Without the Bible, we would be unaware of the historical rootage of our faith. And even the intimations of deity which come to us through general revelation would be difficult to interpret, since our basic vocabulary for describing the activity of God in this world comes from the Scriptures.

This is not to imply that Christian teaching must invariably consist of verse-by-verse biblical exposition. Of course not. There are occasions when this would be singularly inappropriate. One could hardly expect five-year-old children to fathom the meaning of the Beatitudes presented in undiluted form.

Moreover, it is possible to teach the words of Scripture without teaching their central message, just as it is possible to teach biblical truths without reciting the words of the text.

The curriculum of Christian instruction might be likened to the ripples which form on the surface of a pond when a stone falls into the water. The waves move out in concentric circles, some farther from the center than others; but they all radiate from a common point of origin. The specific goals of Christian teaching are numerous and varied, but they ultimately find their origin in biblical revelation.

We conduct mission-study groups because we learn from the Scriptures that Jesus commissioned his followers to "go into all the world" making disciples. We teach units of study in ecology because the Bible teaches that "The earth is the Lord's and the fulness thereof," and that the Creator intends for human beings to exercise dominion over the natural order, not to destroy it. We train Christians in personal evangelism because we read the command of the Risen Lord, "ye shall be my witnesses." We lead seminars on such subjects as abortion, euthanasia, and world hunger, because the teachings of Scripture will not let us ignore them. In these varied ways, the Bible is the touchstone of all Christian teaching.

Christian Teaching Occurs in a Unique Context

One of the most significant statements in the New Testament, relative to the nature of Christian teaching, appears in Colossians 3:16-17.

> Let the word of Christ dwell in you richly, as you teach and admonish one another in all wisdom, and as you sing psalms and hymns and spiritual songs with thankfulness in your hearts to God. And whatever you do, in word or deed, do everything in the name of the Lord Jesus, giving thanks to God the Father through him.

This passage reiterates what has already been said, that the church's educational function is centered in the person of Christ and rooted in his word. The "word of Christ" here refers to the teachings of Jesus, perpetuated by these early Christians through oral and written tradition. It is synonymous with the "all that I have commanded you" of the Great Commission (Matt. 28:20).

But the word of Christ is not merely something to be recited and discussed. It is to "dwell" among them. "Dwell" is the verb used in 2 Corinthians 6:16, "as God hath said, I will dwell in them, and walk in them; and I will be their God and they shall be my people" (KJV).

Paul employs the term to describe the indwelling of the Spirit in Romans 8:11. And in 2 Timothy 1:5 the same word appears in a reference to Timothy's sincere faith, which "dwelt first in your grandmother Lois and your mother Eunice." What this text tells us, then, is that the message of Christ, the subject matter of the congregation's teaching, was not merely a collection of verbal propositions. It was the word of Christ incarnate, a dynamic word, embodied in the lives of individual believers and in the corporate life of the Christian community.

What it means for the word of Christ to dwell in the congregation at Colossae is reflected in verses 12-15. They are to clothe themselves in such virtues as compassion, kindness, lowliness, meekness, patience, forbearance, and forgiveness (Col. 3:12-13). They are to "put on love, which binds everything together in perfect harmony," and let the peace of Christ rule in their hearts (vv. 14-15). And in this context the congregation as a whole becomes a context for education in the faith, as its members "teach and admonish one another in all wisdom" (v. 16).

In other words, the congregation is the laboratory of learning in which the word of Christ is taught, not only by verbal instruction, but also by living example, as members of the community of faith teach and learn from one another.

Paul places a similar emphasis on the corporate nature of the church's educational function in Ephesians 4:11-16. Here he speaks of the role of apostles, prophets, evangelists, and pastor-teachers in equipping the saints for the work of ministry and building up the body of Christ. His next words, "until we all attain to the unity of the faith and of the knowledge of the Son of God," make it clear that his primary frame of reference is not the development of individuals, per se, but the schooling of the congregation as a whole. There are individual teachers and learners, to be sure. But the Christian community as a whole is also both teacher and learner. Christian teaching is the business of the whole body of Christ, not just a few of its members.

Christian Teaching and Educational Theory

Because Christian teaching presents the claims of the gospel and seeks life-transforming commitments, because it is centered in a unique person and rooted in a unique word, it stands apart from all other kinds of education.

This means that Christian teaching differs from instruction in algebra, biology, and English literature, even if the teachers of those subjects happen to be Christians. There are many followers of Christ who teach in public and private schools. What they are doing is eminently worthwhile, and it might even be done with a sense of Christian mission. But it is not Christian teaching unless it conforms to the three criteria set out in the preceding section.

The notion that Christian teaching is merely the wedding of general educational methodology to religious subject matter is erroneous. Unless the instructional process is carried out in conscious dependence upon the person of Christ, with a sense of personal commitment to the authority of his Word, even Bible study may be something less than Christian teaching.

But, granted the uniqueness of genuine Christian

teaching, we must now look at the other side of the coin. For, to insist that Christian teaching is distinctive is not to deny that it has much in common with other kinds of teaching.

Christians have every reason to approach the teaching-learning transaction with confidence, knowing that the Holy Spirit is at work in the process. Unfortunately, this very conviction is sometimes the source of shoddy preparation and irresponsible thinking concerning the teacher's task.

Some Christian teachers seem to feel that the Spirit will magically override the disastrous effects of poor planning, erroneous interpretation, haphazard methodology, and boring procedures. What they fail to take into account is that the Spirit works through the psycho-sensory processes which are embedded in human nature, not in opposition to them, and not apart from them.

Consider a high schooler who attends world history classes during the week and a Bible class on Sunday morning. She doesn't suddenly become a spiritual Cinderella, an other-worldly kind of learner, the moment she walks into a Bible class. She will go on sensing, perceiving, conceptualizing, and assimilating information in much the same way, regardless of the particular learning environment. The social climate of the classroom, the nature of the learning activities, and the relationship of these to her own developmental needs will influence her behavior in the Bible class, much as they do in a history class. And her Bible teacher can ill afford to be indifferent to these elements in the learning process.

Teaching methods are not intrinsically "Christian" or "non-Christian." Jesus used probing questions in his teaching, but so did Socrates and Confucius. He told stories with dramatic effect, but Aesop was famous for this technique too. Christian teachers select methods from the arsenal of techniques shared in common by all teachers. For example, a teacher of cultural anthropology might use a cross-cultural simulation game to point up basic elements in human societies. And a Christian teacher might use the same simulation game to demonstrate the meaning of culture shock in the experience of missionaries. To employ this method effectively, both teachers must go to the same sources and learn from the same experts in the field of educational simulation.

The principle holds true in the use of instructional media. There is a right way and a wrong way to utilize an overhead projector in the classroom; and failure to do it right is no more excusable in Sunday School than it is in a vocational training course. And the "talking head" approach to closed-circuit television production is a shortsighted use of the medium, whether the subject matter is general science or general revelation.

Christian teachers have a legitimate place in the larger fellowship of women and men whose lives have been dedicated to the improvement of teaching and learning. These include practicing teachers, subject-matter specialists, instructional technologists, researchers, and educational theory builders. Representing widely variant educational philosophies, pedagogical approaches, and religious attitudes, they share a common devotion to the task of teaching. They do not always agree, but they learn from one another. Even though Christian teachers are motivated by distinctive objectives and rely upon unique spiritual resources, they too can benefit from the common fund of knowledge generated by this broader community of educators.

Unfortunately, this fund of educational knowledge has yet to be recorded and utilized systematically. Through the years, numerous teachers have shared their thoughts on pedagogy with others. Since the late nineteenth century, experimental researchers have patiently explored the nuances of human learning behavior in laboratory and classroom settings. Articles on teaching and learning have appeared by the thousands in magazines and journals. Taken as a whole, the literature on teaching has been voluminous, but fragmentary. Hopefully, it will one day be synthesized into a systematic, integrated theory of teaching.

Actually, little was said about a theory of teaching during the first half of this century. Pschologists were more concerned about theories of learning. If it could be discovered how organisms (human or otherwise) learn, they thought, we could then teach according to that knowledge. E. L. Thorndike (1874-1949) influenced a generation of educators with the learning theory which he postulated in his landmark volume, *Animal Learning* (1898). The intervening years have produced a steady succession of learning theorists, some of them building on Thorndike's "laws," and some quite at odds with his basic paradigms.

By the 1960s, some educators were pointing out that learning theory needed to be complemented by a theory of teaching. Learning theory describes only one-half the teaching-learning process; and understanding the learning process is not quite the same thing as knowing how to influence it. For example, one might understand that certain conditions affect attitudinal changes without knowing how to set up such conditions in the classroom. Or, again, one might know that a sense of achievement can be a powerful motivator in learning without knowing how to capitalize on this in the development of a teaching plan.

Jerome Bruner put his finger on the essential difference between learning theory and instructional theory when he pointed out that theories of learning are descriptive, while a theory of instruction is prescriptive. Learning theory seeks to explain a learning process after it has happened; instructional theory seeks to tell how one may cause the learning to happen (or, at least, to heighten the probability that it will happen).[5]

According to Bruner, a theory of instruction should specify: (1) the experiences which create a predisposition toward learning; (2) the ways in which a body of knowledge should be structured so that it can be most readily grasped by the learner; (3) the most effective sequences in which to present the materials to be learned; and (4) the nature and pacing of rewards and punishments in the process of learning and teaching.[6]

It takes little imagination to appreciate the potential value of a "theory of Christian instruction" conforming to Bruner's specifications. How valuable it would be for someone to come up with clear answers to such questions as these: What are the boundaries of the body of knowledge with which we are concerned in Christian teaching? How should Christian knowledge be structured so as to be grasped most effectively? In what sequences, and at what levels of personal and spiritual development, should various aspects of Christian knowledge be presented to learners? What may be done to stimulate an eagerness for learning among those who participate in church study programs?

The term "educational theory" in the heading for this section was chosen instead of "instructional theory" because "educational theory" has a broader meaning. One writer has described educational theory as "the whole enterprise of building up a body of rational principles for educational practice."[7] Given this definition, the term includes not only instructional theory and learning theory but also ideas from specialists in instructional technology, teacher-training, and educational philosophers as well.

Educational theory might be thought of as "educators in conversation with one another." The conversation is far from finished; education still abounds with unanswered questions. We have yet to see the emergence of a well-knit theory of teaching. What can be learned from educational research is inconclusive. (Only the naïve permit themselves the luxury of citing existing educational research with dogmatic rigidity.) The question, What is good teaching? has yet to be answered definitively. And, as a matter of fact, there are a great many educators who question whether or not teaching can ever be reduced to an exact science, preferring instead to see it as a performing art. But it is important to continue the conversation, if for no other reason than that it helps us formulate the questions which need answering.

Summing Up

All that has been said in this chapter rests on two fundamental convictions.

First, Christian teaching is like no other teaching because it calls for a quite specific commitment on the part of teachers and learners, is centered in a unique Person, grows out of a unique Word, and takes place in the context of the Christian community.

Second, Christian teaching is like other teaching in that it addresses itself to whole persons (not detached "spirits") whose psycho-sensory processes operate in much the same manner from one learning situation to another, and in that most instructional skills are as relevant to the Christian teacher's work as they are to that of other teachers.

As paradoxical as it might seem to insist, at the same time, on the uniqueness and the sameness of Christian teaching, these two assumptions must be held in tension with one another. To let go of either of these ideas is to distort the nature of Christian teaching.

Notes

1. Ian A. Muirhead, *Education in the New Testament* (New York: Association Press, 1965), p. 15.
2. Floyd V. Filson, "The Christian Teacher in the First Century," *Journal of Biblical Literature,* 60 (1941), p. 318.
3. Burton Scott Easton, "The First Evangelic Tradition," *Journal of Biblical Literature,* 50 (1931), pp. 150-51.
4. Werner Jaeger, *Early Christianity and Greek Paideia* (Cambridge, MA: The Belknap Press of the Harvard University Press, 1962), p. 93.
5. Jerome S. Bruner, *Toward a Theory of Instruction* (Cambridge, MA: The Belknap Press of the Harvard University Press, 1966), p. 40.
6. Ibid., pp. 40-41.
7. Terry Page and J. B. Thomas, *International Dictionary of Education* (London: Kogan Page Ltd., 1979), p. 342.

4
A Christian View of Learning

Socrates was one of history's great exemplars of *maieutic* method in teaching. The term comes from a Greek word which means "midwife." As a teacher, Socrates saw himself functioning as a kind of intellectual midwife, helping his students give birth to the ideas which were already latent in their thinking.

The concept is rich in metaphorical meaning. It places teaching and learning in proper relationship. A midwife and a mother participate cooperatively in the same event; yet their respective roles are different. The midwife's task is to facilitate the birth of a baby; but it is the mother who must actually give birth. The mother depends upon the midwife to make her task easier; but the midwife depends upon the mother to make her work meaningful.

Similarly, a teacher and a learner participate cooperatively in the same event; yet their respective contributions to the teaching-learning transaction are distinctive. The teacher's task is to facilitate learning; but each individual must do his or her own learning. The learner depends upon the teacher to make the task easier; but, without the learner, the teacher's work would be utterly devoid of meaning.

Even though teaching and learning are different functions, they are inseparably related, like the respective tasks of midwife and mother. In this sense, learning may be called "the other side of teaching." To put it another way, learning is the product of teaching, just as good health is the product of a physician's work and bread is the product of a baker's work.

Every good workman is intimately acquainted with his product. It is not enough for a physician to be trained to recognize pathological conditions; she must also be able to identify healthy tissue and normal organic functions. A baker must know good bread when he sees it. By the same token, a teacher should have some understanding of learning.

As noted in the previous chapter, Christian teachers derive an understanding of their task from two primary sources: biblical revelation and contemporary instructional theory. A well-rounded view of the process of learning also takes both of these perspectives into account. While biblical writers approach learning from a unique theological point of view, many of their insights are strikingly compatible with those of modern educational psychologists. The following analysis of learning from a Christian perspective will draw from both of these sources.

A Definition of Learning

Consult a dozen educational psychology books, and you will find almost as many definitions of learning. Like teaching, learning is a rich, complex phenomenon that virtually refuses to be reduced to a single definition. However, most definitions would be compatible with this one: *Learning is a process in which durable changes occur as a result of experience.*

Since, like most definitions, this one is couched in abstract language, it might be useful to unpack it, piece by piece:

Learning as process. "Process" is a key word in our definition of learning. It suggests fluidity, synergy, and continuous interaction among the many elements entering into the experience of the learner.

The ancient philosopher Heraclitus illustrated the meaning of process when he observed that a person can't step into the same river twice, since the ongoing stream is in a continuous state of change. This is true of the learner's "stream of experience." A teacher never deals with the same learner twice, since every human being is in a constant state of growth and flux. What happens in a class is always tempered by what takes place outside the classroom in the life of the learner.

It is especially important for Christian teachers to keep this in mind, since we can so easily persuade ourselves that the "spiritual" nature of a person may be treated in isolation. No one ever comes into a Bible class or church training group out of an experiential vacuum. A learner brings with her all the interests, biases, values, joys, pains, aspirations, grudges, and personal needs which she experiences in the crucible of everyday living. And these have a strong bearing on what she learns and how.

Jesus expressed this principle when, as he explained his parable of the sower, he spoke of "those who hear the word, but the cares of the world, and the delight in riches, and the desire for other things enter in and choke the word, and it proves unfruitful" (Mark 4:18-19).

The word *process* also denotes a holistic view of learning. New learnings don't come into an individual's experience in hermetically sealed units, like golf balls dropped one by one into a bucket. They behave more like cream added to coffee, permeating thoughts and feelings, changing the configurations of the individual's thought structure even as they are changed by it. A powerful new concept can precipitate a reorganization of material previously learned. A newly-acquired attitude interacts with a broad spectrum of existing attitudes, tempering them or strengthening them.

Let me illustrate. I grew up under preaching which tended to fix the experience of salvation at a particular point in time. I often heard individuals refer to "the time when I was saved." In other words, my thinking about salvation was focused on a past event. Years later, I read a book by a New Testament scholar, A. M. Hunter, in which he pointed out that the apostle Paul spoke of salvation in three temporal dimensions—past, present, and future. This new knowledge was not just another brick to be added to the structure of my theology, alongside the thoughts already there. Rather, it altered that structure, modifying and rearranging it, changing my perceptions not only of the doctrine of salvation, but of redemption, sanctification, and discipleship as well.

Learning as change. All learning involves some kind of change. If you haven't changed in some way, you haven't learned. The changes aren't always observable. They may take place within the brain, the glandular system, or the muscles. They may be overt psychomotor development or subtle reorganizations of neural patterns. But, whatever the specific form, change characterizes all learning experiences.

Learning might bring about an increase in the quantity of data stored inside the learner's head but it might also involve a simplification of information. A learner may be taught to organize ideas more effectively, perform physical tasks more efficiently, or feel differently about persons, objects, or ideas. The common denominator in all of these experiences is change.

Thinking of learning as change should help us understand why individuals sometimes resist learning. Change is costly. It requires expenditure of energy. Anyone who has tried to change from the "hunt and peck" system of typewriting to the touch system can attest to that.

Have you ever tried to alter an entrenched habit, or change the way you feel about someone who rubs you the wrong way, or develop a psychomotor skill such as playing the guitar? Then you know that learning tasks like these don't come without a price tag. It is much easier to maintain the status quo, to rest comfortably in a state of peaceful equilibrium, than it is to be changed through learning.

Learning as durable change. A child is able to name the five books of the Pentateuch at the end of a class session, but can remember only two of them one week later. Have the books of the Pentateuch been learned? What if the child is unable to name them only a day later? Or one hour later? Can we say that learning has taken place?

Have you ever been introduced to a group of individuals only to realize, after the usual exchange of pleasantries, that you haven't retained a single name? Did you learn those names?

Obviously, learning can't be defined adequately without some reference to the matter of retention. We can hardly call it learning if students repeat a Latin conjugation as the word forms fall from the lips of their teacher but cannot repeat them later without the teacher's help. That's why the modifier *durable* has been included in our definition of learning.

How long is durable? How long must something be retained before we can say that it has been learned? There is no definitive answer to this question. But, even if we can't answer it, we can at least know some of the reasons why it can't be answered.

In the first place, it is imprecise to ask, "How long must something be retained?" This question doesn't take into account the difference between *recognition* and *recall*. When you meet a group of people, you might fail to *recall* the names even minutes later. But several days later, someone might ask, "Have you ever met Jane Gruble?" and, in a flash of recognition, you remember that Jane was one of the persons you met. It is much easier to learn something well enough to recognize it again than it is to learn it to the level of recall.

Another factor which influences the durability of learning is the similarity of the situation when the material was learned to the one in which it is supposed to be remembered. Suppose, for example, that a teacher orally repeats the names of the books of the Pentateuch until her pupils can say them, then later writes these on the board and asks, "What do we call these five books of the Bible?" In this case, a visual stimulus has been substituted for an audible one; and this would make recall more difficult. Children are not the only learners affected by this problem. Many a college student has heard terms in lectures which she doesn't recognize on a written examination paper.

Closely related to this is the question, Under what conditions are students supposed to demonstrate what they have learned? It is one thing to be able to name the cities of the Decapolis during New Testament times, but it is quite another to be able to point out their locations on an outline map. Reciting a memorized definition of church is not the same as telling what a church is in one's own words.

To take another example, an individual might be able to quote certain Scriptures related to the gospel of salvation in the sympathetic environment of a Bible class, but recalling these same Scriptures in the heat of a discussion with non-Christian business associates is a different matter. The problem in the latter instance is not so much that the Scriptures have not been "retained," but, more than likely, that stressful factors in the situation are interfering with the recall mechanism.

There is yet another complicating factor when we address ourselves to the question, "How long must changes in the learner persist before we can say that learning has taken place?" We cannot always assume that nothing has been learned simply because the learner fails to recall specific details. A person might participate in a study of Isaiah 6:1-8 and, from that time on, have a heightened consciousness of the living presence of God in worship experiences, even without remembering the name of the prophet.

Learning as the result of experience. The last five words in the definition are intended to exclude changes in a person which might result from maturation or physical agents such as drugs. These should not be counted as learning from a teacher's point of view. The learning with which teachers are concerned grows out of personal experience.

The idea that learning is the result of experience opens the door to a possible misunderstanding. Some teachers have a tendency to associate experience exclusively with overt activity, such as touching, manipulating, looking, listening, writing, or smelling. They feel that pupils really aren't learning much unless they are busily engaged in projects, group processes, or creative activities. They refer to such activities as "experiential learning." But, really, all learning is experiential, since all learning results from experience of some kind. And experience covers a lot of territory. It can range from operating a piece of machinery to reading a book, from playing a game to just sitting and thinking private thoughts.

Individuals are related to the world around them primarily through physical sensory channels. But Christian teachers believe that the experiential milieu of the learner also includes spiritual impressions. The "image of God" in human beings means that we have the capacity to respond to God as his divine Spirit touches our human spirit. Jesus Christ said to his disciples, "When the Spirit of truth comes, he will guide you into all the truth" (John 16:13). The Christian teacher claims that promise.

Learning Is More Than Listening

Learning is a complex phenomenon surrounded by misconceptions. For example, many people entertain the erroneous notion that sitting within hearing distance of a teacher's utterances is tantamount to learning. In keeping with this perception of learning, a teacher might say something like this:

"Yesterday we learned that the Archbishop of Canterbury is the spiritual leader of a worldwide community of Anglicans."

What the teacher probably means is that she talked about the Archbishop of Canterbury on the previous day. Her conclusion that "we learned" does not necessarily follow. Such remarks grow out of the assumption that there is an exact equivalence between learning and listening to teacher talk. That assumption is not valid.

The sounds emanating from a teacher's vocal mechanism must leap several hurdles before they become "learning."

First, the auditory signals must be picked up by the learner's primary sensory receptors. (Faulty hearing on the part of the learner, poor articulation on the part of the teacher, or a high noise level in the classroom could interfere with this.)

Second, the learner's sensory cell receptors must transmit impulses to the central nervous system where these signals are screened and given a preliminary interpretation. (Inattention, such as is caused by daydreaming, could kill the message at this point.)

Third, the stimuli in the nervous system must be translated into some kind of meaningful pattern. The meaning grows out of the learner's experience fully as much as it comes from the teacher's intention. The learner might hear "prophesy with liars," for instance, as the teacher reads "prophesy with lyres" from 1 Chronicles 25:1.

Even if the teacher's communication has made its way

through all the potential barriers to this point, it would hardly be accurate to say that learning has occurred. For the message must now be integrated into the learner's cognitive structure and stored in his memory. And this stage of the process is affected by several variables, including the learner's emotional state, self-perception, previous experience, value system, and language skills.

The foregoing analysis, admittedly brief and incomplete, suggests why learning must be regarded as a two-way street, rather than as the passive reception of messages from a teacher. At every stage, the learner should be as actively involved in the process as the teacher is and, in fact, may exert a determinative influence on the final learning outcome. An obvious implication of this is that the teacher must approach her task with a proper sense of humility, because no one can guarantee that learning will happen in accordance with a prepared script (or lesson outline).

Research studies show that participatory learning experiences, such as group discussion, have decided advantages over methods which call only for passive reception. In group discussion, the material learned becomes more meaningful to the learner because he must constantly "improvise," rephrasing the ideas in his own words, rather than merely repeating them as he has heard them. Many studies have demonstrated that learning is internalized to a greater degree where the student has an opportunity to improvise. One reason for this is that discussion lends itself to clarification as individuals explain and reexplain their statements, often discovering areas of vagueness or distortion and correcting them.

Recent research has also shown that the discussion

method produces greater changes in beliefs, preferences, and attitudes than passive types of exposure, and that such learning persists longer. In other words, instructional approaches which treat the learner as more than a set of ears mounted on legs are likely to produce greater understanding and longer lasting learning.

A number of biblical passages seem to recognize the difference between the act of listening and the acquisition of meaningful learning. In Isaiah 6:9f., the prophet receives a divine mandate to preach God's message to an unheeding people who "Hear and hear, but do not understand; see and see, but do not perceive." The word translated "understand" here is the Hebrew *bin,* the original meaning of which was "to distinguish, separate." Over time, the word came to bear a variety of related meanings: "to be clear, to state precisely, to understand."[1] The people would hear the prophet's utterances but would not learn anything meaningful from them.

A similar contrast appears in Daniel 12:8, where Daniel tells about seeing in a vision a "man clothed in linen." After listening to the man's words, he says: "I heard, but I did not understand."

The meaning of *bin* comes across even more clearly in Nehemiah 8, which tells the story of an occasion when the people of Israel were gathered together to hear a reading of the Law. Ezra, the priest, and a group of Levites were in charge of the meeting. "And they read from the book, from the law of God, clearly, and they gave the sense, so that the people understood [*bin*] the reading" (Neh. 8:8). Verse 7 tells us that the Levites "helped the people to understand the law, while the people remained in their places." The passage pictures an instructional situation in which trained teachers took pains to nurture real comprehension.

The contrast between understanding and mere hearing appears in the New Testament also. In 1 Corinthians 14:2, Paul wrote, "one who speaks in a tongue speaks not to men but to God; for no one understands him."

In one of the encounters between Jesus and the Jews presented in the Fourth Gospel, Jesus raised the question, "Why do you not understand what I say?" (John 8:43). In this passage, "understand" translates the verb *ginoskein,* which denoted in ordinary Greek the "intelligent comprehension of an object or matter." Rudolf Bultmann has pointed out that *ginoskein* went beyond mere sensory perception. In contrast to the verb, *aisthanesthai,* (which emphasized instinctive, unreflective perception), *ginoskein* referred to comprehension by means of one's mental capacities.[2] Jesus was telling his detractors that even though they were hearing his words, they were not grasping his meaning. His words were "going in one ear and out the other."

But why were his hearers not learning from him? Jesus answered his own question: "It is because you cannot bear to hear my word." The problem was not unlike what modern psychologists call "cognitive dissonance," a term popularized by Leon Festinger.[3] The basic idea in Festinger's theory is that a person cannot embrace incompatible ideas (or "knowledges") in his thinking without experiencing a tension which must somehow be alleviated. An individual will try to reduce the tension either by rejecting one of the conflicting ideas or by harmonizing them in some way. If, for example, you are tied emotionally to the religious tradition in which you have been reared, but develop a strong interest in a quite different religion, you are likely to experience a tension which can be resolved only by reaffirming your previous faith commitments or by going "all out" for the new religious beliefs. This, essentially, was the dilemma faced by Jesus' hearers in John 8:31-47.

When a new idea conflicts with one already held by an individual, and if the two ideas can't be harmonized, a person will reject the new idea or give up the old one. In the first instance, no learning will have taken place, since nothing will have changed. In the second instance, the new knowledge will have been learned only when the tension has been resolved by displacement of the older idea.

Festinger's "cognitive dissonance" theory explains why people will sometimes actually go out of their way to avoid information which seems incompatible with their previously held beliefs. Even in the face of cogent, well-documented arguments, they will throw up emotional barricades which effectively block out new information rather than rearrange the old belief system. Sometimes learning can be too painful and too costly. Mere hearing is usually less expensive than comprehending.

Transforming Knowledge

The Greeks and the Hebrews had strikingly different conceptions of knowledge. Bultmann has treated this subject at length in his discussion of *ginoskein* in *The Theological Dictionary of the New Testament*.[4] He points out that the Greek contemplated knowledge from a distance, never touching it, lest it become something less than the pure truth. The Hebrew, on the other hand, came to understand the object of knowledge by experiencing it and interacting with it.

Commenting on this contrast between Greek and Hebrew thought, C. H. Dodd wrote:

> Accordingly, for the Greek, to know God means to contemplate the ultimate reality. . . . For the Hebrew, to know God is to acknowledge Him in His works and to respond to His claims. While for the Greek knowledge of God is the most highly abstract form of pure contemplation, for the Hebrew it is essentially intercourse with God; it is to experience His dealings with men in time, and to hear and obey His commands.[5]

The verb *yada* reflects the Hebrew attitude toward knowledge as well as any other term in the language of the Old Testament. Early in the biblical record we read, "and you will be like God, knowing [*yada*] good and evil" (Gen. 3:5). *Yada* denotes a way of knowing which goes beyond the mental processes. It has to do with experienced knowledge. Thus, a woman "knows" the pain of childlessness (Isa. 47:8). The "Suffering Servant" of Isaiah 53:3 "knows" the anguish of sickness (the word "acquainted" in the KJV and RSV being a translation of *yada*).

Through Jeremiah the prophet, God says, "I will make them know, this once I will make them know my power and my might, and they shall know that my name is the Lord" (Jer. 16:21). Obviously, the "knowing" spoken of here entails something other than a bookish lesson in theology. The people will know divine punishment as one knows the sting of a lash.

A mildly amusing incident related in 1 Samuel 14:12 further illustrates the experiential nature of the knowledge denoted by this term. Jonathan and his armor-bearer, scouting out the Philistine forces, are spotted by enemy soldiers. "Come up to us, and we will show you [*'cause you to know'*] a thing," the Philistines call out to them, with obvious bravado. What they have in mind is obviously something a bit more existential than the transmission of verbal information.

This Old Testament conception of knowledge permeated Jewish thinking during the New Testament era and even beyond. Even though memorization was a necessary mode of learning in a day when there was little written material, the rabbis were strongly opposed to any learning which went no further than cramming facts into the head and reciting them with mechanical monotony. Concerning this, Birger Gerhardsson has written:

> They criticized with both humor and irony those who had memorized great masses of textual material without understanding what their own mouths were saying. They compared such persons to magicians who mumbled formulas which they do not understand, or to lifeless baskets filled with scrolls.6

The point is not just that the rabbis were anxious for their disciples to understand what they learned. It went beyond that. They wanted their students to *live* what they learned.

> According to the rabbis a disciple ought not to be a dead

receptacle for the received tradition. He should rather enter into it so that he understands it and is in agreement with it. Only thus can he actually live according to it, be a fruitful steward of it, and pass it on to others in an infectatious way. A living bearer of the tradition is to be like a torch which has been lit by an older torch, in order that it might itself light others.[7]

Jesus and his followers, like the prophets of the Old Testament and the rabbis of the New Testament period, placed a premium on experiential learning.

Luke described an occasion when a nameless woman in the crowd surrounding Jesus "raised her voice and said to him, 'Blessed is the womb that bore you, and the breasts that you sucked!' " But Jesus' response made it clear that he was more interested in obedience than in flattery: "Blessed rather are those who hear the word of God and keep it" (Luke 11:27).

In the Great Commission, a small word, easily overlooked, brims with significance. The word is "observe." Omit it from Matthew 28:20, "teaching them to observe all that I have commanded you," and the nature of the church's teaching mission is radically altered. The Greek infinitive (*terein*) means "to keep," "to watch over," "to preserve," "to fulfill," "to pay attention to," and "to observe."[8] Obviously, Jesus did not intend for his teachings to be reduced to a collection of dull recitations. The unanswerable question recorded in Luke 6:46 makes this abundantly clear: "Why do you call me 'Lord, Lord,' and not do what I tell you?"

Early Christians shared the Hebrew conviction that learning should penetrate to the center of personality and be woven into the warp and woof of daily experience.

One of the most powerful statements of this truth in the New Testament is the exhortation in Romans 12:2, "Do not be conformed to this world but be transformed by the renewal of your mind, that you may prove what is the will of God, what is good and acceptable and perfect." In Paul's writings, the word *nous* ("mind") includes the intellect, the functions of knowing and understanding; but it also encompasses a much broader meaning. The *nous* also embraces the will, the seat of moral judgment which determines what is to be done and what is not to be done. As Bultmann has written, "Just as there is no willing and planning without knowing and understanding, so for Paul, knowing-and-understanding is everywhere of the sort that plans something, that contains an aim toward action."[9]

In other words, "renewal of the mind" might very well begin with the thought processes, with knowing and understanding; but it leads to nothing less than transformation of personality and revitalization of life itself. This is the ultimate goal of Christian teaching.

Notes

1. 1. Helmer Ringgren, *"bin; binah; tebbunah,"* G. J. Botterweck and Helmer Ringgren, eds., *Theological Dictionary of the Old Testament,* Vol. II (Grand Rapids, MI: William B. Eerdmans Publishing Co., 1977), p. 99.

2. Rudolf Bultmann, *"ginosko,"* Gerhard Kittel, ed., *Theological Dictionary of the New Testament,* Vol. I (Grand Rapids, MI: William B. Eerdmans Publishing Co., 1964), p. 690.

3. Leon Festinger, *A Theory of Cognitive Dissonance* (Stanford, CA: Stanford University Press, 1957).

4. Bultmann, *"ginosko,"* p. 690.

5. C. H. Dodd, *The Interpretation of the Fourth Gospel* (Cambridge: Cambridge University Press, 1954), p. 152.

6. Birger Gerhardsson, *The Origins of the Gospel Traditions* (Philadelphia: Fortress Press, 1979), p. 24.

7. Ibid.

8. William F. Arndt and F. Wilbur Gingrich, *A Greek-English Lexicon of the New Testament and Other Early Christian Literature* (Chicago: University of Chicago Press, 1957), p. 822*f.*

9. Rudolf Bultmann, *Theology of the New Testament,* Vol. I, trans. Kendrick Grobel (New York: Charles Scribner's Sons, 1951), p. 212.

5
The Content of Christian Teaching

The 1960s produced a plethora of innovations in education. Programmed instruction and dial-access retrieval systems soared into prominence on the wings of advancing technology and federal funding. New school buildings were constructed without interior walls. Media centers supplanted old-fashioned audiovisual-aids storage closets. Overhead projectors became as prominent as chalkboards in some schools, and low-cost videotaping brought a powerful new learning tool into the classroom. Interactive teaching methods complemented the mood of the counterculture. And new terminology—"modular scheduling," "autotelic learning," "individually prescribed instruction"—filtered into the official vocabulary of educators.

A burgeoning emphasis on behavioral objectives challenged the ambiguities of foggy instructional aims. Teaching strategies magnified student initiative and deemphasized traditional approaches to discipline, not always with happy results. In many quarters, "discovery learning" took precedence over traditional expository methods in the classroom.

By the mid-1970s, a great many parents who had been

brought up on "readin', writin', and 'rithmetic" had become convinced that these newfangled innovations were ruining education. They suspected that many of the learning activities in their children's schools were generating more activity than learning. And these doubts were not entirely without foundation. Some "schools without walls" fell flat on their faces. Colleges turned out a generation of graduates who didn't know how to spell or read a book. "Creativity" became a euphemism for articulate ignorance.

The mounting anxieties of parents and other concerned citizens created a powerful urge to plunge headlong into the past, where "schools were schools" and teaching was a straightforward, no-nonsense business. This reactionary mood gave rise to the "traditional school," built on a philosophy of stern discipline, hard work, and time-honored curricular offerings. By the dawn of the 1980s, traditional schools had sprung up all over the country and were attracting applicants in great numbers.

One of the rallying cries of those who became disenchanted with educational innovation was, "Give us more content!"

Witness this excerpt from a letter written to me by a religious educator serving on a local church staff:

> In perhaps the time of greatest educational methodology advancement, we see content suffering immeasurably. The public schools here in our area are beginning to rue the day content was sublimated [sic] to methodology. Students finish school learning little as a result of relational study and lacking in basic skills and tools.

The content-vs.-methodology controversy surfaces from time to time in church education, too. Many a Sunday School teacher has heard disgruntled parents react to activity-centered teaching methods. ("I bring my children to church to learn the Bible, not to cut out paper dolls and play games.")

The writer of the letter mentioned above had this to say about teaching in the church:

> In our religious education, we must teach the principles of God's work first, and follow with appropriate application—but first things first. May we not realize too late that our new approaches have the form but deny the power thereof—the *content* [italics mine] of God's inspired Word.

Understanding Biblical Content

How are we to understand this "content of God's inspired Word"? Is it necessary only to read the printer's ink impressions on the pages of a favorite translation of the Bible? Or do we also need the Spirit-breathed thoughts which enlighten the mind of a devoted Christian who reads the Bible? Didn't Jesus teach that the illumination of the Paraclete would always be operative as his disciples in all ages continue to reflect on his teachings (John 14:25; 16:13-15)? The inspiration of the Holy Spirit is essential as we seek to understand the content of biblical revelation, apply it, and adjust our life-styles accordingly.

During those dark years when the clouds of World War II threatened to engulf Great Britain, Alan Richardson wrote, "only the mind which has learnt to read the language of the Bible can understand what God is saying in the events of these stirring days." Then he went on to say:

> Christians have always believed (and always will believe) that God speaks through the Bible to their hearts in every age; they do not think of the Bible as a message which God wrote several centuries ago. . . . They think rather of God still speaking through the Bible to men. Thus, the Bible is not the record of a dead revelation, but the living medium of a present revelation.[1]

Was Richardson speaking of the "content of God's inspired Word" when he referred to "a present revelation"? It would be difficult to think otherwise.

And what about the feelings that arise—feelings of reverence, thankfulness, joy, or contrition—as one ponders the words of Scripture? Surely such emotional responses are further indications of the work of the Holy Spirit in us as we appropriate into our lives the "content of God's inspired Word." Has a person mastered the *content* of Isaiah 6:1-8 when she learns to recite, discuss, or exegete the passage? Or would "content learning" in this instance also include a personal sense of the presence of the Lord, like that which the prophet experienced?

Has one learned the *content* of John 15:12 when he is able to "explain the passage in his own words"? Or, would it be more correct to say that he has not truly learned the content of this passage until he is able to exemplify love toward fellow Christians in his personal relationships with them?

What that religious educator meant when he spoke of the "content" of God's word was precisely what academicians mean when they speak of "content courses." They mean words, of course. Linear, abstract, verbal formulations. The more abundant the flow of words, the greater the "content."

And, of course, in the world of theological education the opposite of the "content" course is the "practical" course. Thus, systematic theology is a "content" course, but church administration is "practical." Church history deals with "content," but pastoral counseling with "practice" (notwithstanding the volumes of verbatims and case studies which might be written by students in the latter course).

The same bias is present today in church education, where the recited word seems somehow to be more substantive than the enacted word, where propositional truth takes precedence over intuitive experience, and where many seem to feel that the only Bible content worth learning is that which can be appropriated through the left hemisphere of the brain.

So long as the terms *content* and *content learning* continue to be bandied about as mere labels for orderly patterns of words, questions concerning content in Christian teaching are likely to generate more heat than light. Those who wish to "view with alarm" the alleged subordination of content to methodology would do well to decide exactly what it is they think is being subordinated.

Content and Method

It makes little sense to pit method against content, as though these terms were completely at odds with one another. Method and content are not mutually-exclusive concepts. In actual practice, they can't be separated.

In the teaching-learning situation, method inevitably becomes a part of the content, just as subject matter becomes a determinant of method. The two flow together. There can be no content without method, no message without a medium. Anything that is taught at all must be taught by some kind of method. The teacher who decides to present biblical material by lecturing on selected passages is employing a method no less than a teacher who depends upon a filmstrip or dramatization to convey the message.

The content of any message is determined not only by the information which it carries but also by the treatment of the information. If a person makes three statements, but says one more loudly than the others, this treatment implies that the one statement is more important than the other two; and this implied emphasis becomes a part of the content.

Consider the message, "Oh, I hate you!" On the basis of the words alone, we might reasonably assume that this is intended to be a hostile communication. But, spoken by a coquettish young lady, with exaggerated gestures and inflections, the message might even convey affection. In both instances, the basic information is the same; the treatment makes the difference in content.

A teaching method is, among other things, a way of handling material to be learned. And the handling of it always has something to do with shaping the content. A teacher might lecture to a social studies class, saying: "In a three-tiered society, where lower, middle, and upper classes are sharply stratified, the people in the lower class often feel helpless, frustrated, and angry, because they find it impossible to control the forces which shape their lives."

On the other hand, the teacher could involve class members in a simulation game in which they actually play the roles of persons in a three-tiered society, a game which is so rigged in favor of the "haves" that the "have-nots" finally throw up their hands in utter frustration and say, "The rules aren't fair! We aren't going to play anymore!" Then the teacher might kick off a discussion by asking, "Do these feelings give you any insight into the causes of racial riots in large cities?"

In the simulation, the students don't just hear information; they feel it as to some degree they experience the anger and frustration of people who have been disenfranchised by society. In each of these teaching strategies, the basic information would be essentially the same; but the *content* would be different because of the differences in methodology.

Those who fret about the "subordination of content to method" in public schools and in church education have not defined the problem correctly. The problem which concerns them is not really that there is too much method and too little content. What they are really worried about is the apparent discrepancy between the content (including subject matter and methods) and their presuppositions concerning the nature of education. In other words, the issue has to do with *kinds of content,* not the relative amounts of content and method.

Content and Knowledge

What, exactly, is content? Some would say, "Well, you teach content when you concentrate on the body of knowledge to be mastered." But this explanation isn't very satisfying, since "knowledge," like "content," is a moving target, ever changing its configurations in the very process of being known.

Knowledge is never merely "received." The learner responds to data coming in from the environment by manipulating it, remodeling it, combining it with previous experience. And, in this way, knowledge is fashioned even as it is communicated. As the learner assimilates it, knowledge becomes an amalgam of external stimuli and personal experience. In other words, the learner does not just absorb new information as it comes to him. He adds something to it even as he receives it.

Have you heard that story about a father who took his seven-year-old son to see the Grand Canyon? For some reason, the mother had to stay home. In a few days, she received a letter from her husband and a card from her son. Her husband described the lovely panorama of variegated hues splashed against the canyon walls by the golden glow of a radiant sunset. The little boy wrote, "Dear Mom, I spit a mile today!"

Which had truly come to know the Grand Canyon? In one sense, the boy's report was the more objective of the two reports; the father's description was colored by his own internal responses and romantic language. Both had been exposed to the same visual stimuli, but what each had actually perceived was determined in part by his unique set of predispositions.

When subject matter of any kind is presented to a group of learners in a church educational setting, some pay attention, some do not. Some see and hear, some do not. The incoming signals stick in the sensory registers of some, but, with others, they "go in one ear and out the other." Each person filters the information through her own perceptual screen, evaluating and coding it in light of her unique background. If the material seems important, the learner will store it in her memory, attaching it to some category of data already there. During the process, a dozen learners might translate information into "knowledge" in a dozen different ways, just as a group of children in a crafts class can start with identical materials, follow the same pattern, yet turn out uniquely different creations.

Picture a group of women engaged in a study of Ephesians 5:21-33, a passage which includes the exhortation, "let the wife see that she respects her husband." One class member enjoys an ideal relationship with an emotionally mature, loving husband. But another is married to an alcoholic who turns into a beast every weekend, abuses the children, stays out of work most of the time, and steals objects from the house in order to raise enough money to buy cheap booze. It is most unlikely that the Scripture text will convey the same meanings to both women. What they come to know of the Bible passage during this study session will be shaped by what they already know of life.

The Calcification of Content

It is widely believed that the "content" of education is synonymous with verbal material, written or spoken, and that methodology is merely the technique of transferring words efficiently from teacher to learner. This notion continues to be one of the most insidious debilitating influences in the practice of religious education today. "Insidious," because it seems so right to so many. "Debilitating," because it constitutes a denial of emotional, relational, and experiential aspects of learning.

What this concept of education leads to is aptly illustrated by an episode in Charles Dickens's novel *Hard Times.* The episode takes place in an English schoolroom. The main characters are little Sissy Jupe (daughter of a circus equestrian, a rider and trainer of horses), Bitzer (the star pupil in Sissy's schoolroom), and Mr. Thomas Gradgrind (the schoolmaster). After some preliminary discussion concerning the occupation of Sissy's father, which leaves her thoroughly confused, Gradgrind asks her to give a definition of "horse." Though Sissy has ridden and taken care of horses for as long as she can remember, at the moment she is frightened speechless.

"Girl number twenty unable to define a horse!" says Gradgrind. "Girl number twenty possessed of no facts, in reference to one of the commonest animals! Some boy's definition of a horse. Bitzer, yours."

Bitzer rises to the occasion. "Quadruped. Graminivorous. Forty teeth, namely twenty-four grinders, four eye-teeth, and twelve incisive. Sheds coat in the spring; in marshy countries, sheds hoofs, too. Hoofs hard, but requiring to be shod with iron. Age known by marks in mouth." Thus (and much more) Bitzer.

"Now girl number twenty," says Gradgrind, "you know what a horse is."[2]

In Dickens's tale, Bitzer is a veritable paragon of "content-centered" learning. Although the story is a parody, exaggerated out of proportion, it does make the point that something is lost in the translation of living experience into words. When detached from first-hand experience, verbal content has a tendency to calcify—that is, to "change into a hard, stony substance."

And this invariably happens when Christian teaching becomes just a matter of transferring words, and nothing more.

Findley Edge described the problem succinctly in his book *Teaching for Results:*

> As the learner progresses from childhood, through youth into adulthood, teachers use words to teach him religion. . . . As he comes to Sunday School regularly, through the years, and learns and accepts the words which describe religious experiences, he tends to identify this with having had the experiences. That was precisely one of the problems Jesus encountered with the religion of the Pharisees. They verbalized about the great teachings of the prophets, but they had not learned the spirit of these teachings in their experience. How much this is happening in our Sunday Schools today! Learning words which describe a religious experience is not the same thing as having the experience.[3]

The Word of God was intercepting human personalities on the plane of daily existence long before it was cast into written symbols. This living word permeated emotions, altered values, revitalized relationships, and transformed lives.

Moses encountered the flaming bush that refused to burn up while doing his daily stint as a herdsman in the Sinai wilderness. Hosea developed a deeper understanding of the God of Israel in the crucible of broken family relationships. Simon, James, and John were plying their trade as fishermen when Jesus came along; and Levi met the Master as he sat at his tax-collector's table.

The opening words of 1 John make it clear that the experienced Word preceded the written record of that Word: "We write to you about the Word of life, which has existed from the very beginning. We have heard it, and we have seen it with our eyes; yes, we have seen it, and our hands have touched it" (v. 1, GNB).

The writer of the passage goes on to say why he is verbalizing this experience: "What we have seen and heard we announce to you also, so that you will join with us in the fellowship that we have with the Father and with his Son Jesus Christ" (v. 3, GNB).

This inspired writer's purpose was to transform relationships, to redeem lives, to bring others into the sphere of an overwhelming experience; not to provide material for mental gymnastics in church school sessions.

Verbal symbols provide a vehicle for the preservation and communication of biblical tradition. But if Christian teaching begins and ends with the transmission of biblical words, and nothing else happens, the biblical revelation will not have come to its full fruition.

Striking a Balance

Now, having dwelt at length on the folly of reducing the Word to mere words, let us circle around and approach the subject from the other side. For there is another side. Just as some have attempted to communicate biblical content without regard to method, others have focused attention on method to the exclusion of biblical content.

A case in point is a "Bible class" (to use the term

loosely) which I visited one bright Sunday morning. With a membership consisting of young adults, most of them college and seminary students, the class was trying very hard to be nontraditional. Arriving a few minutes early, I browsed around the room. In one window I found a package of Sunday School lesson quarterlies, apparently unopened, and a few copies of a mimeographed "Class Schedule." The first topic on the schedule was "Helping Ministries in Our Community." The next four topics were "Understanding Transactional Analysis." After that, the program chairperson apparently had run out of ideas, because the rest of the Sundays on the schedule were devoted to "Sharing." Later, after the class meeting, I asked a member, "What do you share on these Sundays?" She paused a moment, then said, "We just, you know, we just share."

At that point, I was beginning to sympathize with the viewpoint of the religious educator mentioned earlier in this chapter. "In perhaps the time of greatest educational methodology advancement, we see content suffering immeasurably." Christians certainly should not be indifferent to helping ministries in the community. Discussing transactional analysis was, at least at that time, an interesting pastime. And who would argue against the need for "sharing" in a community of Christians? But, at least from the church's point of view, Bible study was this group's reason for being. And, whatever else might be said about these activities, they were something less than Bible study.

One of my basic presuppositions as a religious educator is that the Bible must occupy a central place in all Christian teaching and learning. Its writings constitute the primary documents of our faith, so much so that it is impossible to understand the Christian faith apart from the text of the Bible. I fervently believe what Alan Richardson expressed so forcefully when he wrote:

> What we are saying is that God *does* speak to men through the Bible, that the Bible is the medium of His message to the world, that the Bible is God's own appointed channel of communication with men. That is to say, the *normal* order of things is that man hears God speaking to him as he kneels with the Bible in his hand. If God speaks to men through the Church, that is because the Church is the place where the Bible is read, or it is the community which listens to the public reading of the Bible. If God speaks to men through the sacraments, that is because they are sacraments of the Bible-drama. If God speaks to man in the sermon, that is because the Bible is preached. If God speaks to men in prayer, that is because the prayer is the prayer of the Bible. And if God speaks to men through nature, or through things which are lovely and characters which are noble, that is because they have learnt from the Bible the accents of His voice. The Bible is and remains the appointed means of God's conversation with men.[4]

The church must teach the Bible, for the people of God will not comprehend who they are, or what their message is, if they do not understand the Scriptures. Nor will individual believers understand their unique calling as disciples of the Lord Jesus Christ, if they are unacquainted with this word of truth. Christians must study the Bible. This task includes reading the Bible devotionally as well as studying its text analytically. Obviously, we must give attention to the words of the biblical text, weighing them, discussing them, even memorizing them.

What I have emphasized in this chapter, however, is that the content of Bible study need not be restricted to verse-by-verse exposition, or to the language of favored versions.

Some Christians are so bound to the language of some particular Bible version, they write threatening letters to editors who dare to print the words of another version. Yet, ironically, they follow a Master who often used metaphors drawn from life to communicate the Word of God, rather than relying exclusively upon the sacred language of Scripture. Jesus sometimes quoted the prophets. But, more often, he spoke of seeds, birds, flowers, winds, lost coins, lamps, salt, and houses built on rock and sand.

If biblical truth is to penetrate the understandings of today's hearers, we must continue to develop new metaphors to serve as vehicles for the divine message, just as Clarence Jordan did when he turned Ephesians into "The Letter to the Christians in Birmingham" in his "Cotton Patch Version." When biblical truth is clothed in such powerful contemporary symbols, this too is a way to teach "the content of God's inspired Word."

In Western culture, we have inherited an educational tradition which places almost exclusive emphasis on the kinds of learning associated with the left hemisphere of the brain, the side which controls our logical, abstract, verbal, analytical thought processes. Research in recent years has called attention to the role of the right half of the brain, the side which has to do more with imaginative, creative, aesthetic, metaphorical thinking and experiencing.[5]

To illustrate the difference between these two kinds of learning, consider the familiar passage in Isaiah 40 which begins, "Comfort, comfort my people, says your God." You might analyze the passage with the aid of a biblical commentary, giving special attention to its historical context. Or you might have your heart lifted and your mind filled with inspiring imagery as you listen to the words of this passage set to music in Handel's oratorio, *Messiah*. The first experience would be of the kind primarily associated with the functions of the left hemisphere of the brain, the second with the right hemisphere. The "content" of biblical revelation could be learned through both of these quite different experiences.

Christian teachers should strike a happy balance between these two modes of thought when designing learning experiences. While we need very much to be skilled in the communication of truth through artistic, imaginative, symbolic, intuitive learning experiences, it would be most unfortunate for us to deny logical, analytical thought modes in the process. We will never reach the whole person if we abolish the left side of the brain any more than we can educate whole persons while denying the existence of the right hemisphere.

While advocating a renewal of interest in right-brain learning in Bible study, Walter Wink warned against going to the extreme in this direction, thus denying the importance of the more verbal and logical intellectual capacities:

Truth would not be served if in our recoil from the

one-sideness of left-brain domination we plunged head-long and heedlessly into the right. That way lies real danger. Many today, especially intellectuals, having so long denied this other dimension, discover its voices and capitulate to them altogether. Others, predisposed to anti-intellectualism, are susceptible to the allure of a subjective, uncritical, uninformed exegesis, one capable of confirming them in their warm feelings about themselves, but having little power to renew their minds.[6]

In other words, Christian teachers should never let "activity teaching" degenerate into sheer activity. Nor should mere relating be passed off as relational Bible study. And it should be acknowledged that making collages, participating in group conversation, and engaging in role play do not necessarily produce meaningful learning, if they are not used discriminatingly.

But, on the other hand, let us never fall prey to the seductive notion that listening is the same as understanding, that labeling is the same as experiencing, and that the content of Christian teaching and learning can be reduced to verbal formulas.

E. Stanley Jones, one of the famous missionaries of our generation, stood before a seminary chapel audience at the beginning of the Christmas season a few years ago. He preached on the text, "And the Word became flesh" (John 1:14). Toward the conclusion of his message, he said, "The world never understood what God was trying to say until the Word became flesh. Mind you, the text does not say, 'The Word became *words*.' The Word must become *flesh* again and again, if it is to be understood by a sinful humanity."

The Word made flesh is the ultimate content of Christian teaching and learning.

Notes

1. Alan Richardson, *A Preface to Bible Study* (Philadelphia: The Westminster Press, 1944), pp. 15,23.
2. Charles Dickens, *Hard Times* (Greenwich, CT: Fawcett Publications, Inc., 1966), p. 28.
3. Findley Edge, *Teaching for Results* (Nashville: Broadman Press, 1956), p. 16.
4. Richardson, p. 15.
5. Walter Wink, *Transforming Bible Study* (Nashville: Abingdon Press, 1980), pp. 21-25.
6. Ibid.

6
The Role of the Christian Teacher

A university freshman met an aging professor as he walked across the campus one morning. Stopping squarely in front of the student, the old gentleman pointed a bony finger at him and said, "Young man, what excuse do you have for existing today?"

Teachers sometimes ask themselves such questions—that is, if they take their teaching seriously. It's easy enough to engage in pedantic skyrocketry, deriving enough satisfaction from the sound of your own voice to make it all seem worthwhile. But if you seriously regard teaching as a way to help persons learn, there are times when you wonder, "Are my teaching activities really influencing the learning process all that much?"

After all, a lot of learning takes place without benefit of teachers. Consider the incessant learning activities of infants and little children, finding out about their world through self-initiated exploration—grasping, inspecting, tugging, pushing, pulling, and taking things apart. They learn social behavior by mimicking parents, older children, and peers. To a great extent, they teach themselves.

Then, of course, there's the learning that takes place in front of that ever-present electronic guru, the television. Commenting on the educative power of TV during the preschool years, Marshall McLuhan once quoted an IBM executive as saying: "My children had lived several lifetimes compared to their grandparents when they began grade one."[1]

People continue to learn on their own initiative through adolescence and adulthood. My brother, for example, worked with sophisticated electronic equipment in a voice-sciences laboratory for fourteen years without ever having taken a course in electronics. What he knows about electronics (quite a lot, actually) he picked up without the aid of a teacher, by reading, tinkering, and experimenting. Similarly, a department manager in a large aluminum plant prepared himself for a changeover to computerized operations by working his way through self-study manuals. And a great many Christians have learned what they know about the Scriptures through personal Bible study.

A team of Canadian educational researchers found, after having conducted extensive surveys in several countries, that it is not uncommon for adults to spend from 500 to 700 hours a year in major learning efforts, but that about 73 percent of all adult learning projects are planned by the learner, without the help of a teacher.[2]

Where, then, do teachers fit into the picture? Is teaching really "a relatively unimportant and vastly overvalued activity," as Carl Rogers once wrote? Is teaching unessential to learning? Or does the teacher fulfill a role which is significant, and even indispensable?

My own point of view is that the teacher serves as an important catalyst in the learning process. A catalyst, you may recall, is an agent which accelerates a chemical reaction. Strictly speaking, the catalyst does not cause the reaction, but it does facilitate it so that it happens faster and with greater intensity. And this can be a very crucial function.

Your body, for instance, could conceivably transform ingested food into new protein without the aid of the catalysts called enzymes, but the process might take years instead of minutes. Similarly, almost any intelligent person could learn without the assistance of a teacher; in the presence of effective teaching, however, learning takes place faster and in greater quantity. Were it not for teachers, it is doubtful that anyone could acquire essential learning fast enough to survive in an increasingly complex world.

What does a teacher do to help the learning process along? To put the question in the vernacular of small children, "What are teachers *for?*" The rest of this chapter is a response to that question.

The Teacher as Motivator

Where I grew up as a small-town boy, childhood wasn't so regimented as it is today. We didn't have to spend Saturdays playing Little League ball for the entertainment of parents and coaches. So, on many a Saturday morning two or three of us kids would find ourselves sitting on somebody's front porch trying to think up a way to have fun without getting into trouble. The sitting around didn't last long, though, when Harold was with us. He had a knack for thinking up exciting things to do. In no time at all, he could have us fixing up a clubhouse in someone's backyard shed, or setting out, equipped with our Daisy BB guns and peanut butter sandwiches, to Little River. Harold was a motivator. He could turn lethargy into activity and channel idle energies into constructive projects. He knew how to make things happen.

Christian teachers need to have that quality, the ability to make things happen. People often show up in classrooms without any particular sense of purpose. Teachers know from experience that members of church learning groups aren't always propelled by a burning desire to learn something new. Some come out of a sense of duty, some because of family expectations, and others because they enjoy the social contacts. Even those who have a vague desire for learning don't know clearly what they want to learn. So, having no learning goals in mind, they don't pursue them. They need someone to help them find a reason for learning.

Motivation might be thought of as the release of potential energy for specific purposes. All of us have latent energy stored in the cells of our bodies, and we must draw upon these reserves for everything we do, whether washing dishes, walking, thinking, or even lying at rest.

Since energy is available in limited supply, we are naturally conservative with it, expending no more than we have to. But we will spend it on things that seem worthwhile. For instance, writing this book is hard work, and during the course of an evening I can find dozens of excuses to get away from my word processor. But I keep putting out the energy demanded by the task, because I am highly interested in it. In other words, I am motivated.

Think about the meaning of this in an instructional situation. Learning can be hard work. When you call upon learners to solve problems, work with pencil and paper, participate in discussions, or even listen attentively, you are asking them to expend energy. And you must help them find a good reason for doing so, or it won't happen.

When a person mobilizes the energy stored up in the cells of his body, he usually does it in order to meet a need of some kind. One summer, when I plowed up a bumblebee's nest in my garden, I released a tremendous burst of energy because I suddenly felt an urgent need to move my body to a different location. The sense of need is often more subtle than that, but nonetheless real. For instance, the need to solve riddles, answer provocative questions, and satisfy curiosity is deeply implanted in human personality, and we sometimes spend appreciable quantities of energy on such tasks.

If learning activities aren't related to the felt needs of learners, they will expend as little energy as possible on these activities. This explains why students sometimes slump in their chairs, doodle on writing pads, stare at the ceiling, look out the window, and lapse into complete silence. On the other hand, a sure way to get learners "turned on" is to introduce learning tasks that speak to personal needs. ("Turned on" is, of course, a slangy expression which American language inherited from the youth culture of the 1960s. But it describes rather accurately what happens when learners become motivated. They literally "turn on" the energy stored in the cells of their bodies.)

But motivation isn't just a matter of coaxing learners to release their energies. It also involves releasing learners, freeing them from the influences which tend to inhibit learning, such as feelings of self-doubt, naivete, and incompetence. No one wants to look foolish in front of other people. But that is the risk a person takes when he engages in group study activities. Have you ever noticed how embarrassing it is for someone to be called upon to read a Bible passage aloud when he can't pronounce the words? Do you know people in learning groups who invariably remain silent rather than risk giving an opinion which might not meet with approval? Have you observed boys in middle adolescence who would sooner die than participate in classroom dramatizations or other activities calling for personal creativity? Often as not, the reason for such reticence is the fear that they won't be able to "cut it" in front of the group. Nonparticipation is better than looking stupid.

No one wants to fail. No one wants to seem ignorant. And few people are willing to give up the security of previously-held ideas. This is the reason there are Christians who seem not to have experienced a new theological pattern in twenty years. Familiar ground is comfortable; untraveled paths are threatening. Teachers, as motivators, will try to minimize the influence of such obstructions to learning.

As a teacher, Jesus was a master motivator. He had an extraordinary ability to engage individuals at the point of their personal needs, to stimulate curiosity, to start where they were and lead them to where they ought to be.

The Gospel narratives abound with examples. In the opening chapter of the Fourth Gospel, we find a description of an early encounter between Jesus and two disciples of John the Baptist. Observing that the two were following him, Jesus turned and asked, "What do you want?" (John 1:38, NIV). (Motivation for learning always runs at a higher level when teachers take time to ask this simple question, "What do you want?" rather than launching immediately into what they want to present.) Probably not knowing what to say, on the spur of the moment they responded by asking, "Where are you staying?" Jesus replied, "Come, and you will see."

At this point, the Teacher was using one of the best of all devices for motivating learners: curiosity. (Unskilled teachers often make the mistake of answering questions directly; experienced teachers recognize the value of creating enough uncertainty in the minds of learners to let them search for answers.) The lesson that day was long. It was also highly successful, judging from what one of the learners said to his brother: "We have found the Messiah" (John 1:41). What a wasted opportunity it would have been had Jesus simply told these two men his street address.

Another example of Jesus' ability to stimulate significant learning appears in the same Gospel. In his conversation with the Samaritan woman at Jacob's well (John 4:6-26), Jesus refused to be sidetracked into a discussion of mundane religious issues. He penetrated to the core of the woman's greatest personal need (vv. 16-19). (Researchers have discovered that personal needs precipitate more learning efforts among adults than any other motivator.) Again, the lesson was highly productive. The woman left her water jar at the well, hurried into the city, and said to the people, "Come, see a man who told me all that I ever did. Can this be the Christ?" (vv. 28-29).

Paul, too, had the instincts of a good teacher. He knew how to start where his hearers were, leading them from the familiar to the unfamiliar. His encounter with the philosophers on the Areopagus is a prime example. He had already noticed numerous religious shrines and images in the city, and he used this as his point of departure when responding to their question, "May we know what this new teaching is which you present?" (Acts 17:19). He began by saying, "Men of Athens, I perceive that in every way you are religious. For as I passed along, and observed the objects of your worship, I found also an altar with this inscription, 'To an unknown god' " (vv. 22-23). Then he said, in effect, "I can tell you who that unknown God is." What Greek listener, with a finely-tuned sense of curiosity, could have kept from paying attention? Though Paul could not have known it, he was establishing what a contemporary instructional theorist has called "a predisposition toward learning."[3]

The Teacher as Guide

The lake was large and unfamiliar, a maze of coves, inlets, and small islands. It was good to have a guide along, a fellow who knew where he was going. We would come to a place which to an untrained eye had no distinguishing characteristics, and the guide would say, "We'll find some crappie here." And we would. When the action slowed down, he would take us to another spot.

The work of a guide parallels the task of teaching in some ways. For instance, this guide knew the territory. He had spent years on the lake exploring every cove and inlet. He knew where to find the deep channels, rocky points, and caves in the sandstone bluffs. Similarly, a teacher must know the way around in the subject matter.

Jesus once said some scathing things about "blind

guides," teachers of the law whose knowledge of the law was shallow and distorted (Matt. 23:24). Those blind guides have contemporary counterparts, would-be teachers of the faith whose knowledge of the subject matter is less than adequate. They are like the "certain persons" described in 1 Timothy 1:6-7 who have "wandered away into vain discussion, desiring to be teachers of the law, without understanding either what they are saying or the things about which they make assertions." At best, such teaching is uninspiring; at worst, it is misleading and confusing. A person who doesn't know the way can't function as a guide. One cannot teach what one does not know.

The well-known story of Philip's encounter with the Ethiopian eunuch in Acts 8:26-39 paints a picture of a situation in which a skilled teacher functions basically as a guide.

The learner is highly motivated by his quest for religious truth—so much so, that he has already been searching the Scriptures on his own. The teacher is highly competent in his knowledge of the subject matter; and he is led by an intense desire to help the learner appropriate the truth of the gospel. The one-on-one teacher-pupil ratio is ideal. The instructional method is dialogical, with ample opportunity for a free-flowing exchange between teacher and learner.

A crucial turning point in the narrative comes in verse 31, where the Ethiopian responds to Philip's question, "Do you understand what you are reading?" He looks up from the scroll containing the prophecy of Isaiah and responds, "How can I, unless some one guides me?" The verb "guides" (*odegeo*) suggests the picture of a shepherd leading his sheep. The term is used in a pastoral sense in Revelation 7:17, where it is written that the Lamb will be a shepherd who will feed his people, and will "guide them to springs of living water." This same word also appears in Jesus' statement concerning the function of the Paraclete in John 16:13, "When the Spirit of truth comes, he will guide you into all the truth." In a very real sense, Philip was used as an instrument of this same Paraclete to guide his Ethiopian pupil in an earnest search for truth.

Because the quest for truth in Christian education invariably hinges upon the guidance of the Spirit, being in touch with the Spirit is an indispensable qualification for the Christian teacher. No matter how astute one might be in technical knowledge of the Scriptures, he will prove to be a "blind guide" if he is not alive to the Spirit's leadership and illumination.

A guide's main function is to show the way. On the fishing trip mentioned earlier, we might have wasted the day groping our way around unfamiliar shorelines and squandering bait in unproductive waters without the services of a guide. Unguided learning effort can be terribly inefficient; it entails so much random search behavior. Learning by trial and error is time-consuming and often demoralizing. The task of the teacher is to point the way, identify areas for productive study, and help learners avoid dead ends. Finally, it might be worth noting that after showing us where and how to fish, our guide let us do our own fishing. It takes all the fun out of fishing and learning when someone else does everything for us.

The Teacher as Resource Provider

You might say a teacher functions as a broker. In the commercial world there are certain people who want to buy certain commodities, and other people who want to sell them. But prospective buyers and sellers don't always know one another; and that's where the broker comes into the picture. The broker's job is to be a go-between for those who have needs and those who can supply them.

A similar situation exists in the world of education. Learners need certain resources, and those resources are often available in abundance; but the people who need them might not know how to appropriate them. A teacher's task is to bring learners and learning resources together.

During one sabbatical study leave, I spent eleven months in Oxford, England, before discovering an agency there which develops and utilizes educational games and simulations. Since educational simulations had been a consuming interest of mine for several years, I certainly would have made it a point to visit this agency had I known of its existence. It was the kind of resource that a teacher might have recommended. But lacking the services of a teacher, I was left to discover the information quite by accident in a book which I purchased the day before my departure from England.

Learners in the church are often in the same predicament. They would like to locate certain Bible passages, but have never discovered how useful a concordance can be for that purpose. Puzzled by biblical terminology,

they are unaware of the Bible encyclopedias and commentaries that could help resolve these difficulties.

During a study of Hosea, someone raises the question,
"Where can I find out more about the Baal worship of
ancient Canaan?" The teacher suggests a Bible dictionary
containing an article on the subject.

A person wants to learn how to use the concordance
in her Bible. Her teacher recommends a self-study book-
let, *Developing Skills for Bible Interpretation.*

To help a youth group visualize the work of missionaries in French-speaking West Africa, a mission study
leader uses an audio slide presentation.

The leader of a workshop for Bible teachers distributes
a bibliography of books related to the process of instruction. In all of these instances, teachers are functioning as
resource-providers.

A well-equipped teacher knows resources. A resource-
ful Bible teacher should be able to identify various commentaries, explain differences between English versions
of the Bible, name several useful commentaries, order
filmstrips pertaining to biblical topics, know where to
find a schematic drawing of the first-century Jerusalem
Temple, locate geographical information on Palestine,
and draw from an extensive repertory of teaching-learning procedures when planning learning activities. A re-
spectable knowledge of resources can make the
difference between prosaic and stimulating study sessions.

But knowledgeability isn't enough. The teacher must
also be a "resource-getter." I once attended a men's
Bible class where the teacher would say, periodically, "If
we had a map of the Bible lands during the time of Jesus

(or of Abraham, Moses, or Isaiah), we could see where.
. . ." I often wondered why that teacher couldn't persuade the church to provide a set of maps for his classroom. I doubt if he ever tried.

The Old Testament account (2 Chron. 34:14-33) of an
episode which occurred during the reign of Josiah, king
of Judah, dramatically illustrates the importance of a key
learning resource. As workmen were renovating the
house of the Lord, Hilkiah the high priest found a scroll
containing "the law of the Lord given through Moses,"
a document which apparently had been long hidden.
When this discovery came to the attention of the king, he
summoned all the elders of the land to Jerusalem. "And
he read in their hearing all the words of the book of the
covenant which had been found in the house of the
Lord" (v. 30). Then the king, and the people, "made a
covenant before the Lord, to walk after the Lord and to
keep his commandments and his testimonies and his statutes" (v. 31). In this instance, a crucial resource was
absolutely essential to the learning situation.

After the scroll was found, Hilkiah gave it to Shaphan,
the king's secretary. Then Shaphan told the king, "Hilkiah the priest has given me a book" (v. 18). And that
statement sums up one of the most important functions
of the teacher. "He has given me a book."

The Teacher as Evaluator

During an early summer Vacation Bible School, I su-
pervised about twenty fifth graders during a creative activities period each day. As my young charges worked
with wood, leather, and ceramics, they continually asked,

"How does this look?" "Is this OK?" "What about this?" "Am I doing it right?"

They were, of course, asking for evaluation—for two reasons. First, these lads really did want to know whether or not they were "doing it right," because they were learning new skills, and weren't quite sure of themselves. But, second, they needed reinforcement, praise for a job well-done. Evaluations offered by teachers serve both purposes. Teachers both guide and reward learning effort through evaluation.

Evaluation is an important component of teacher-learner interaction in all kinds of instructional situations. A novice golfer swings a driver, and the instructor says, "That was much better; but keep your head down." An elementary school pupil works an arithmetic problem on the board, then turns to the teacher with a "Did I get it right?" look on his face. A member of a Bible class asks, "Wouldn't this be an example of a 'theophany'?"; testing his knowledge of the concept. Students frequently ask, "Have our papers been graded yet?" because they are eager for an assessment of their performance. Even when a student is working through a self-instructional program without the direct supervision of a teacher, evaluation plays an important role in the process as each successive frame tells the student whether or not her previous response was correct.

Evaluative feedback is an indispensable adjunct to practice. Practice alone does not make perfect. To rehearse the pronunciation of a biblical name 100 times could mean that it has been repeated incorrectly that many times, unless a teacher is present to judge the accuracy of each attempt. Improvement comes only through evaluated practice.

Skilled teachers know how and when to offer evaluation. Too little evaluation leaves learners wondering whether or not they are doing OK. Too much evaluation stifles learning activity and lowers morale.

Evaluative feedback was very much a part of the teaching practice of Jesus. At Caesarea Philippi, he posed the question, "Who do you say that I am?" (Matt. 16:15). Simon Peter responded, "You are the Christ, the Son of the living God." And Jesus said, "Blessed are you" (vv. 16-17). Later, Peter said something to Jesus that brought a harsh response from the Teacher: "Get behind me, Satan! You are a hindrance to me" (v. 23). In the first instance, Jesus used evaluation to reinforce an idea that needed to be remembered. In the second, his feedback corrected an erroneous interpretation of his messianic mission.

Evaluation is closely related to a function which has been assigned to teachers since ancient times—the task of correction. Correction figured prominently in ancient Jewish instruction. Hebrew educational thinking related invariably to the concept of the Law as the ultimate standard of conduct and belief. The Law was to the Hebrew what a compass is to a ship; and the purpose of instruction was to help the individual stay on course. This educational aim appears early in Genesis: "I have chosen him [Abraham], that he may charge his children and his household after him to keep the way of the Lord by doing righteousness and justice; so that the Lord may bring to Abraham what he has promised him" (18:19).

Correction was often achieved through stern disciplinary measures. Significantly, the Hebrew term which most often denotes "instruction" in the Old Testament (the verb *yasar* and its nominal cognate *musar*) also means "to chasten" or "to discipline." Thus, corporal punishment was seen as being essential to the educational experience of growing children. "He who spares the rod hates his son, but he who loves him is diligent to discipline him" (Prov. 13:24; cf. Prov. 22:15). The educative influence of the rod might even save the life of a child (Prov. 23:13-14). The need for corrective discipline is by no means limited to children. Adults, too, were admonished not to "despise the Lord's discipline or be weary of his reproof, for the Lord reproves him whom he loves, as a father the son in whom he delights" (Prov. 3:11-12).

This concept of instruction through corrective discipline appears also in the New Testament, particularly in Hebrews 12:5-11. The Greek term *paideia* (or the verb *paideuo*) appears no less than nine times in this passage. The term is typically translated "correction," "discipline," or "chastening." The association of the word with harsh corrective discipline is dramatized by Pilate's use of *paideuo* with reference to the cruel scourging of Jesus (Luke 23:16).

But if *paideia* sometimes denoted physical punishment, it was never *mere* punishment. Whatever *paideia* involved, its purpose was always educational.

Paideia, in fact, was one of the great educational concepts of ancient Greek culture. In its earliest and most primitive form, *paideia* (and the verb *paideuein*) had to do with the "upbringing and handling of a child which is growing up to maturity and which thus needs direction, teaching, instruction and a certain measure of compulsion in the form of discipline or even chastisement."[4] (Both words were built on the stem, *pais,* "child.") But During the fifth century BC, *paideia* took on a much broader significance. It stood for the whole educational process by which character was shaped according to the finest expectations of Greek culture. The goal of *paideia* was achievement of *arete* ("virtue" or "moral excellence"), a comprehensive ideal encompassing the individual's character, citizenship, and intellectual life.[5]

According to this classical concept of education, the Greeks thought of teaching (*paideuein*) in terms of "the formation of man" (*morphosis*). This notion presents a picture of the gradual shaping of personality and character, not unlike the process by which a sculptor works with a lump of plastic clay to form an image.[6] To pursue the analogy further, the sculptor forms the pliable clay according to a pattern which he already has in mind. In Greek education, that pattern was determined by the whole corpus of Greek literature, beginning with Homer; but, more specifically, by philosophy. In fact, philosophy, as Plato conceived it, eventually became identical with *paideia* in its most developed form.[7]

Jaeger and other interpreters have drawn significant parallels between the Greek concept of *paideia* and aspects of early Christian education. As in the case of *paideia,* the purpose of Christian teaching is the shaping of the individual according to an ideal pattern. The pattern is Christ himself; Christ must take shape within the believer. Christians are urged to attain to the "knowledge of the Son of God, to mature manhood, to the measure of the stature of the fulness of Christ" (Eph. 4:13).

In Christian teaching, the Bible takes the place of Greek literature as the believer's *paideia*. Gregory of Nyssa, one of the foremost Christian thinkers and writers of the fourth century, was an ardent advocate of this concept of Christian education. He contended that the formation of the Christian man, his *morphosis,* is the effect of his unceasing study of the Bible. He repeatedly referred to the biblical authors as educators. But their pedagogical authority was derived from the Holy Spirit, who inspired the writing of the Scriptures. Therefore, it is the Spirit who is the real educator.[8]

This excursion into the classical meaning of *paideia* in ancient Greek culture sheds light on a New Testament passage which reflects the original meaning of the term, "the upbringing of children." In Ephesians 6:4, fathers are told, "do not proke your children to anger, but bring them up in the discipline [*paideia*] and instruction [*nouthesia*] of the Lord." Commenting on this passage, Bertram has said, "Here the basic rule of all Christian education is stated. . . . this is the education which the Lord gives through the father."[9]

This Scripture is full of significance for Christian teaching. In the first place, it fixes responsibility for nurturing children in the faith squarely on the shoulders of Christian parents, and more specifically on fathers. Second, it lets us know that the Christian upbringing of children involves more than the mere sharing of information. Both *paideia* and *nouthesia* make this clear. While "instruction" is an appropriate translation of the latter term, it doesn't quite convey the full force of the word, which also carries the meaning "warning" or "admonition." And, in keeping with the preceding discussion, *paideia* conveys the idea of shaping or forming the child in the pattern of Christ. This may be done through a variety of methods including instruction in the Scriptures, setting an example, controlling, guiding, and exercising discipline in love.

And there is one other tremendous truth here. As Bertram points out, the parent doesn't merely do this in the name of Christ, or tell the child things about Christ. Christ himself is the child's educator; and the father serves as the Teacher's aid in this process.

But Bertram is exactly right. We have in this passage "the basic rule of all Christian education." All Christian teachers are in the business of shaping character, of molding personality, of helping individuals grow toward "the measure of the stature of the fulness of Christ." And they are called to be participants in the educational process which originates with the Master Teacher.

The Teacher as Exemplar

Volumes have been written about the teaching methods of Jesus. The Master Teacher did utilize a wide-ranging repertory of teaching strategies; but his disciples learned most by observing and following his example. Jesus was a personification of the kingdom of God, a living model of his teachings. His disciples came to understand what "love thy neighbor as thyself" meant as they saw how he related to others. He didn't merely lecture about the attributes of God, he demonstrated the nature of God in a personal way. "He who has seen me has seen the Father," he said (John 14:9). Looking back on their experience in the school of Christ, his disciples would later say, "And the Word became flesh and dwelt among us" (John 1:14).

These words constitute a profound doctrinal affirmation; but they also hold significant educational implications. The Word became not *words,* but flesh. Words are important vehicles of truth in Christian teaching, but Christian teaching can never be reduced to words alone. Somewhere in the process the words must become flesh. They must be translated into personal characteristics, social behaviors, and emotional responses, if they are to strike their targets in the hearts and minds of learners. Otherwise, they will not be understood. Words are abstract symbols. They derive their meaning ultimately from concrete experiences. It is not enough merely to define words like *love, forgiveness,* and *faith;* someone must demonstrate these attributes if these words are to become flesh again.

The Christian teacher must know the message. But, more than that, the teacher must *be* the message. The apostle Paul knew this quite well. For this reason he urged Christians at Corinth, "Be imitators of me, as I am of Christ" (1 Cor. 11:1). At first glance, this demand seems presumptuous, perhaps even conceited. But Paul might well have been the first Christian ever to be seen by many of the Corinthians. Thus, it was logical, even inevitable, that he should become their exemplar in the faith. The significant thing is that Paul recognized the importance of what modern psychologists call "modeling" as a means of teaching the Christian way of life.

An individual who learns by observing the behavior of another person (a model) and patterning his own behavior accordingly is learning by "imitation." This kind of learning is a well-known phenomenon, probably one of the most important in human experience. It is exemplified by learners who take pains to copy the forehand swing of a tennis instructor, by a baby who learns how to use a spoon by watching her mother go through the motions of eating strained spinach, and by children who learn the routines of worship by observing what their parents do in church. (Learning through imitation is also exemplified by small children who witness the temper tantrums of adults in their homes, then beat the stuffing out of dollies—and other children—while "playing house.")

Occasionally, seminary students have been known to develop the mannerisms and voice characteristics of favorite professors or preachers. This illustrates the power of learning through imitation. And just let a hallowed professional football player exhibit a behavioral idiosyncrasy, such as "spiking" the ball in the end zone or doing a quaint little victory dance after a touchdown, and the new behavior soon becomes standard practice on gridirons everywhere, all the way down to the peewee leagues.

Psychologist B. R. Bugelski has said that imitation is "probably the greatest single, and most widely practiced, operation in learning and in all human activity."[10] Clearly, learning by imitation is too important to be ignored in the process of Christian education. This means, of course, that the role of the teacher as a Christian model must be taken seriously. *Who a teacher is* can either complement or negate what she says. A person who is unloving, pessimistic, soured on life—no matter how "correct" doctrinally he might be—will hardly inspire learners to celebrate the joy which is theirs in Christ. One who is bored with, and burdened by, the task of teaching is not likely to kindle enthusiasm among class members. On the other hand, a teacher whose personal faith has been refined in the crucible of pain or personal loss can do more to help learners appropriate the spirit of Psalm 23 than can the most sophisticated commentary on the passage.

Christian teaching is knowing, saying, relating, and doing. But it is also being. The *being* of the teacher authenticates all the rest.

Notes

1. Marshall McLuhan, *Understanding Media: The Extensions of Man* (New York: Signet Books, The New American Library, 1966), p. ix.
2. Allen Tough, *The Adult's Learning Projects,* Second Edition (Austin, TX: Learning Concepts, 1979), pp. 172-73.
3. Jerome S. Bruner, *Toward a Theory of Instruction* (Cambridge, MA: The Belknap Press of the Harvard University Press, 1966), p. 41*f.*
4. Georg Bertram, *"paideuo,"* Gerhard Kittel, ed., *Theological Dictionary of the New Testament,* Vol. V (Grand Rapids, MI: William B. Eerdmans Publishing Co., 1968), p. 596.
5. Additional information on *paideia* was taken from Bertram's article and from Werner Jaeger, *Early Christianity and Greek Paideia* (Cambridge, MA: The Belknap Press of the Harvard University Press, 1962); William F. Arndt and F. Wilbur Gingrich, *A Greek-English Lexicon of the New Testament and Other Early Christian Literature* (Chicago: University of Chicago Press, 1957) pp. 105, 608*f.;* and Werner Jaeger, *Paideia: The Ideals of Greek Culture* (3 vols.) (Oxford: Basil Blackwell, 1961).
6. Jaeger, *Early Christianity and Greek Paideia,* p. 87.
7. Ibid., p. 91.
8. Ibid., pp. 92-3.

9. Bertram, p. 624.
10. B. R. Bugelski, *The Psychology of Learning Applied to Teaching,* Second Edition (New York: The Bobbs-Merrill Co., Inc., 1971), p. 132.

7

Christian Teaching as Calling

The God of the Bible is a teaching God, and this is not just a metaphor or figure of speech. Time and again in the writings of the Old Testament the Lord is depicted as the Educator of Israel.

In Deuteronomy 4:1, God addresses the people: "And now, O Israel, give heed to the statutes and the ordinances which I teach you, and do them."

In the ancient story of Job, Elihu extols God's greatness: "Behold, God is exalted in his power; who is a teacher like him?" (Job. 36:22).

The prophets also knew God as the Teacher of Israel. Isaiah said to the people of Jerusalem, "Your Teacher will not hide himself any more, but your eyes shall see your Teacher" (Isa. 30:20). And the psalmist refers to the Lord as "He who teaches men knowledge" (Ps. 94:10).

The consistent testimony of Old Testament writings is that God has chosen to reveal himself to humankind through the agency of teaching. It would be difficult to overstate the importance of this concept in the religion of ancient Israel. In an idyllic portrait of a future age,

Isaiah prophesied, "The earth shall be full of the knowledge of the Lord as the waters cover the sea" (Isa. 11:9).

This concept of the the Lord's direct involvement in the teaching of his people has its counterpart in the New Testament in the sayings of Jesus concerning the instructional role of the Holy Spirit: "But the Counselor, the Holy Spirit, whom the Father will send in my name, he will teach you all things, and bring to your remembrance all that I have said to you" (John 14:26; see also 16:13-15).

In the Bible, teaching is consistently regarded as a primary category of communication in the divine-human dialogue. The biblical record also attests to the fact that the Lord called others to be co-workers with him in this task. In the same sense that pastors are "under shepherds" (the point being that they are subordinate to Christ, *the* Shepherd), God called individuals throughout biblical history to be *"under teachers."*

In this chapter we will examine the task of Christian teaching as a divine calling, beginning with the Old Testament literature and continuing through the New Testament. And we shall see that, far from being a routine activity designed to keep children entertained, teaching is a fundamental ministry to which God calls members of the body of Christ, and for which he provides special gifts.

The Parent as Teacher in the Old Testament

God was the Teacher of Israel, but he called parents to function as co-workers in this educational task. From the days of Abraham onward, Hebrew parents understood that they were under a divine mandate to instruct their children in the way of the Lord.

> Only take heed, and keep your soul diligently, lest you forget the things which your eyes have seen, and lest they depart from your heart all the days of your life; make them known to your children and your children's children—how on the day that you stood before the Lord your God at Horeb, the Lord said to me, "Gather the people to me, that I may let them hear my words, so that they may learn to fear me all the days that they live upon the earth, and that they may teach their children so" (Deut. 4:9-10).

The curriculum of this family-based instruction was twofold. First, parents were to retell the story of God's activity in the nation's history. As Redeemer, the Lord had brought the Hebrews out of Egyptian bondage. As Provider, he had seen them through the perils of the wilderness. As Conqueror, he had led them into the Promised Land. The recital of this divine history was of critical importance, for no generation must be allowed to forget how the mighty hand of God had intervened in the lives of his people.

The psalmist provides a glimpse of this educational tradition:

> Give ear, O my people, to
>   my teaching;
>   incline your ears to the words
>   of my mouth!
> I will open my mouth in a
>   parable;
>   I will utter dark sayings from

of old,
things that we have heard and
known,
that our fathers have told us.
We will not hide them from their
children,
but tell to the coming
generation
the glorious deeds of the Lord,
and his might,
and the wonders which he has
wrought (Ps. 78:1-4).

Then, of course, the child must know the law; for the law was considered to be the very voice of God, and the parent must serve as the channel through whom the child would come to understand the divine will. Nowhere else in Old Testament writings is this parental responsibility made any clearer than in Deuteronomy 6:4-9. With reference to this ancient exhortation, Sherrill has written: "One passage has embedded itself in Jewish consciousness more deeply, perhaps, than any constitution or similar document has ever been woven into the mind of any Gentile people, namely, the 'Shema.' "[1]

Fathers were generally regarded as the teachers of their children in Hebrew society. But, by the time the Book of Proverbs was written during the third or fourth century, mothers too shared in this responsibility. The ancient wisdom writer provides clues to this in Proverbs 1:8 and 31:1.

The call to teach was concomitant with other responsibilities of parenthood in ancient Israel. Just as modern parents understand that giving birth to children includes feeding and caring for them, parents in Old Testament days took it for granted that they were to educate their sons and daughters in the faith.

Early Christians seem to have adopted a pattern of family education similar to that of the Jews. Children were nurtured in the faith by their parents. There is no clear evidence that children were ever taught in meetings of the gathered congregation during the earliest years of the Christian era. But we do know of several documents written toward the end of the first century urging upon parents the importance of teaching their children "in the Lord."[2]

The Teaching Priests of Israel

If Hebrew parents taught their children, who instructed parents? The task of educating the Israelites was delegated to a special class of teachers, the priests and the Levites, early in Hebrew history. It was only natural that they would be expected to function in this role, since they were charged with the responsibility of keeping the law secure.

Toward the end of Moses' career, shortly before the Israelites went in to claim the Land of Promise, he emphasized the importance of this priestly duty:

> And Moses wrote this law, and gave it to the priests the sons of Levi, who carried the ark of the covenant of the Lord, and to all the elders of Israel. And Moses commanded them, "At the end of every seven years . . . when all Israel comes to appear before the Lord your God at the place which he will choose, you shall read this law before all Israel in their hearing. Assemble the people, men, women, and little ones, . . . and that they may hear and

learn to fear the Lord your God, and be careful to do all the words of this law, and that their children, who have not known it, may hear and learn to fear the Lord your God, as long as you live in the land which you are going over the Jordan to possess" (Deut. 31:9-13).

This charge to the tribe of Levi is reiterated in the passage commonly referred to as "the blessing of Moses," where he says: "They [Levites] shall teach Jacob thy ordinances, and Israel thy law" (Deut. 33:10*a*; cf. Lev. 10:11).

The priests and Levites continued to be educators of Israel for generations to come, even to post-Exilic times. During the reign of Jehoshaphat (c. 849-837 BC), a group of priests and Levites became itinerant teachers. Accompanied by certain "princes" from the king's court, they "went about through all the cities of Judah and taught among the people," using "the book of the law of the Lord" as their text (2 Chron. 17:7-9). Under Josiah, two centuries later, the Levites were still known as teachers of all Israel (2 Chron. 35:3).

Nehemiah 8:5-9 indicates that the Levites continued to be regarded as teachers even after the return from Babylon. This passage describes an interesting educational event in which Ezra the scribe read the law from a wooden pulpit "in sight of all the people," after which the Levites seem to have circulated among the assembled people, helping them comprehend what they had heard. "And they read from the book, from the law of God, clearly; and they gave the sense, so that the people understood the reading" (v. 8).

Even the prophets, who themselves functioned as

teachers, regarded the priests and Levites as teachers of the people. Malachi, for example, warned the priests of his day to keep faith with the covenant which the Lord had made with the house of Levi (Mal. 2:6-7). "For the lips of a priest should guard knowledge, and men should seek instruction [*torah*] from his mouth, for he is the messenger of the Lord of hosts" (v. 7).

The Scripture just cited brings us back to an important truth. The teacher in Old Testament times, whether parent or priest, was always "the messenger of the Lord of hosts." The teacher was a commissioned representative of God, who continued to be the Teacher of Israel.

Teaching and Prophecy

A contemporary preacher was reading the "valley of dry bones" passage from Ezekiel 37. Each time he came to the verb "prophesy" (vv. 4, 7, 9, 12), he would translate it "preach," for the benefit of his audience, treating the two verbs as exact synonyms. A more accurate translation for "prophesy" would have been "teach." For the Hebrew term is *naba,* which, according to a standard Hebrew lexicon, originally denoted "religious ecstasy," but later came to mean "essentially religious instruction, with occasional predictions."[3]

It is strangely paradoxical that the prophetic function is so universally identified with preaching, as we know it today, rather than with teaching. For the prophets were known in Israel as charismatic teachers. While the priests and the Levites served as instructors primarily in connection with the Temple worship services, the prophets traveled throughout the land and taught the people, emphasizing such themes as social justice and peace.[4]

There is some evidence, in Old Testament references to "bands" or "companies" of prophets, that there were actually "schools of the prophets" in which the prophets systematically instructed their younger disciples. While this evidence is inconclusive, it seems safe to assume that the prophets did provide instruction in the knowledge and skills needed by those who were called to the prophetic profession.

This juxtaposition of prophecy and teaching was only natural, in view of the fact that both functions were rooted in the person of Moses. As one who had met the Lord face to face, Moses was the prophet *par excellence* (Deut. 34:10). As the great lawgiver, who had instructed the people in the divine word received on Sinai, he was the prototypal teacher of Israel.

John Calvin saw this relationship clearly. Explaining Calvin's position, Henderson has written:

> Calvin's conception of Biblical prophets is interesting and crucial. . . . Essentially, he conceived the role of the Old Testament prophet as being twofold: first and foremost, they were seen as guides, expounders of the law, sowers (but not reapers) of the doctrine of the gospel, teachers whose *docendi forma* sets forth Christ; in other words, they perform a didactic office and their doctrine is based on the teachings of Moses, whom Calvin calls the chief teacher (*summus doctor*). Only secondarily and as a kind of textual necessity did Calvin consider the prophetic role of "foreteller" of future events.[5]

A definitive characteristic of the prophet-teachers of the Old Testament was their sense of divine calling. From the time he encountered the voice of God in the burning bush (Ex. 3), Moses lived under a divine mandate to communicate the word of the Lord. The word of the Lord came to Elijah, sending him on a perilous mission to the court of Ahab (1 Kings 18:1). Isaiah, knowing himself to be the Lord's emissary, prefaced his prophetic teachings with the formula, "now the Lord says . . ." (Isa. 16:14a). Jeremiah spoke with the confidence of a man who could say even to hostile hearers, "The word of the Lord came to me, . . . Thus says the Lord" (Jer. 2:1-2). In similar fashion, "the word of the Lord came" to Ezekiel (Ezek. 28:1), Micah (Mic. 1:1), Zephaniah (Zeph. 1:1), Haggai (Hag. 1:1), and Zechariah (Zech. 1:1). The prophecy of Amos is punctuated time and again by the refrain, "Thus says the Lord" (Amos 1:3, 6, 9, 11, 13).

Without exception, the prophetic teachers of Israel operated on the premise that their mission was to help the people appropriate a knowledge of the divine will through faithful and accurate interpretation of the Word of the Lord. They did not initiate their missions; they were sent men. They did not originate the message; they spoke in behalf of Israel's Teacher. They did not step out of the ranks as volunteers; they were called out by the voice of God.

When we examine the educational heritage of ancient Israel, one thing seems clear; from the earliest biblical times, God appointed teachers to be interpreters of his Word—in the home, in tabernacle and Temple, and in wayside gatherings. And those who responded to this divine call played significant roles in the drama of Old Testament history.

The Earliest Christian Teachers

As we have already seen, Jesus came teaching. His mission was unique, of course, for he was uniquely the Word made flesh (John 1:14). But, in one sense, he perpetuated the prophetic tradition of the Old Testament; for his purpose, like theirs, was to reveal the will of God in this world. And, like the prophets, he utilized teaching as a primary operational strategy for accomplishing this goal.

Careful examination of the Gospel narratives makes it apparent that Jesus devoted considerable attention to the preparation of those who would carry on his mission after his departure. By word and example, he trained the twelve to be ambassadors of the kingdom of God. And, as was pointed out in chapter 1 of this book, their preparation included teaching missions under the Master's direction (Mark 6:30).

After his ascension, it was only natural that they would emulate the pattern of his ministry, doing precisely what they had seen their Master do on so many occasions. They functioned as teachers. They taught in the Temple area, in the marketplace, by the wayside, in homes, and in synagogues. Their message was of God; their style was charismatic; their communication was characteristically instructional.

But they taught not just because it was the natural thing to do. They were under divine mandate to teach the Word. The Master had commissioned them to teach all that he had taught them (Matt. 28:19-20). He had assured them that the Paraclete would be available to aid them in the task (John 14:25-26; 16:12-15).

Does this mean that the apostles were called to be specialists in didactic communication, technical experts in the art of pedagogy? The answer is no. The question ignores what has already been said about the nature of Christian teaching (ch. 3). Christian teaching is not a mere technique. It is a communication process that is centered in the person of Jesus Christ, rooted in the Word of God, and devoted to the purpose of leading individuals to life-transforming commitment.

The same question might be raised in connection with preaching. Are preachers called to be specialists in public oratory or classical rhetoric? Not at all. Like Christian teaching, the ministry of proclamation is distinguished by its message, its purpose, and its relationship to Christ. If teaching and preaching are seen as mere technical skills, it is inappropriate to speak of either as a divine calling. But, when both functions are seen in the light of their distinctive Christian characteristics, they may both be viewed as ministries of the Word. Indeed, they frequently occur simultaneously.

Teaching as Calling in the Early Church

Emphasizing the significance of the teaching function in the New Testament church, Floyd Filson wrote:

> The function was essential from the beginning, and in thinking of the earliest years we must avoid the modern tendency to localize the teaching function in men who could not be said to do anything else and could not be called by any other name. Every leader was a teacher, because teaching was indispensable.[6]

Teaching was, indeed, indispensable. But, at first, the

function of teaching seems to have been a shared responsibility. The apostles taught, continuing what they had been doing under the personal direction of Jesus. But they also preached, evangelized, healed the sick, and administered the affairs of the congregation. They did whatever was needed to carry out their apostolic calling.

Paul counted himself an apostle (1 Cor. 1:1). He exercised prophetic functions (1 Cor. 14:37), yet he was a teacher (1 Cor. 4:17). In Acts he is known as an apostle (14:14); but he was named among the prophets and teachers at Antioch (13:1), and his eighteen-month mission in Corinth is specifically described as a teaching ministry (18:11). It is highly probable that this diversification of function was practiced by all the apostles.

Eventually, such functions became more differentiated. Some individuals exercised the gift of prophesy, revealing God's immediate word to the gathered congregation. Some excelled as evangelists, sharing the gospel with persons outside the community of faith. Others demonstrated the ability to teach with power and effectiveness. These became known and respected for their ability to exercise this much-needed gift within the church (see 1 Thess. 5:12-13a, where "admonish" translates *noutheteo,* a pedagogical term).[7]

By the time Paul wrote his Corinthian correspondence (c. AD 54 or 55), teaching had become established as one of the fundamental ministries within congregational life. In his catalog of spiritual gifts in 1 Corinthians 12:4-11, the apostle places "the utterance of wisdom" and "the utterance of knowledge" at the head of the list. Both of these were related to teaching. Commenting on this passage, Brown wrote: "It is striking that, first of all,

Paul mentions gifts that involve the mind, not the emotions (cf. 14:19). The Corinthians placed a major emphasis on gifts involving the emotions. Paul puts first two pedagogical gifts."[8]

Teaching appears among the first three gifts listed in a similar passage in Romans 12:6-8. Here, prophecy and teaching are treated as separate gifts. But it would be reasonable to assume that these two functions were still closely related, even as they were during Old Testament times, since both depended upon the inspiration of the Spirit (1 Cor. 12:8-11).

The distinction between prophecy and teaching might best be understood in relation to their respective bases of authority. The prophet's authority rested on his (or her) sensitivity to the immediate inspiration of the Spirit. The prophet's function was to communicate fresh spiritual insights to the congregation. But teaching involved the twofold function of passing on the tradition (including the *kerygma* and the sayings of Jesus) and interpreting the tradition. So the teacher's authority was derived, in the first place, from the tradition which was so crucially important in the life of the church. But in the interpretation of that tradition, the teacher would often need to depend upon the immediate illumination of the Spirit, since new situations and new issues would require fresh interpretations of the traditions. With reference to this, Dunn has written:

> As the teacher moved beyond the simple passing on of tradition to its interpretation, so the locus of his authority moved more from tradition to charisma. Here his authority is more like that of the prophet than that of the

apostle. As the prophet depended for authority to prophesy on the charisma of faith (Romans 12:6), so the teacher depended for authority to teach on the charisma of teaching (Romans 12:7).[9]

A succinct list of spiritual gifts in Ephesians 4 names apostles, prophets, evangelists, and pastors and teachers. In the Greek text, "pastors and teachers" (v. 11) share the same definite article. This has led interpreters to conclude that both gifts were exercised by the same individuals. Martin has suggested that these "would be local congregational leaders in charge of established churches which had been brought into existence by the preaching of apostles and others."[10]

Later in this same chapter of Ephesians we find another significant reference to teaching in the early church. The readers of the epistle were warned in verse 17, "You must no longer live as the Gentiles do, in the futility of their minds." This is expanded upon in verses 18-19. Then in verses 20-21, "You did not so learn Christ!—assuming that you have heard about him and were taught in him, as the truth is in Jesus." The statement offers strong evidence that Christian instruction was a normal part of the experience of every believer. That they would have been "taught in him" was the expected thing.

On the basis of the New Testament source materials surveyed thus far, it would seem reasonable to make the following generalizations.

First, teaching was an indispensable function in the early church, too important to be left to chance and too crucial to be delegated to unqualified persons.

Second, responsibility for teaching seems to have been

shared by a variety of church leaders, including apostles, prophets, evangelists, and pastors. Whether or not there were persons who were officially designated as "teachers" during the earlier New Testament period cannot be known with certainty; but it seems most likely that certain individuals in the church were recognized and respected for their teaching ability.

Third, teaching was a task to which individuals were divinely commissioned and for which they were equipped by the Holy Spirit. Passages such as 1 Corinthians 12:7-11, Romans 12:6-8, and Ephesians 4:11 strongly imply that the gift of teaching was given selectively to certain members of the congregation, just as other spiritual gifts were bestowed upon others.

After outlining the teaching function within the Pauline churches, Dunn offered the following summary:

> *The teaching function had more the character of "office" than any other of the regular ministries.* For it was constituted not merely by the charisma of the moment but primarily by the tradition of the past. The role of the teacher would therefore almost certainly be limited to those who had ability to retain, understand and teach that tradition.[11]

The Evidence of the Pastorals

The Pastoral Letters, which represent a relatively late period of development in New Testament Christianity, abound with references to the church's teaching ministry.

Titus was told that a bishop "must hold firm to the sure word as taught, so that he may be able to give instruction in sound doctrine" (Titus 1:9). He was exhorted to "teach what befits sound doctrine" (2:1) and to show "integrity, gravity, and sound speech" in his teaching (vv. 7-8).

One particularly interesting passage in Titus is a reference to "older women" who are to "teach what is good, and so train the young women" (2:3-4). Some intepreters have concluded that these elderly women occupied some kind of official teaching office in the church. If so, the instructions given to Titus here fall into the category of what modern Christians might call "teacher training."

Titus 1:10-11 refers to "insubordinate men, empty talkers and deceivers" who upset "whole families by teaching for base gain what they have no right to teach." This reference strongly implies that, at this stage of the church's development, the teaching function of the church was carefully monitored and regarded with utmost seriousness.

A similar expression of concern about erroneous teaching appears at the beginning of 1 Timothy. Here, Timothy was told, "Remain at Ephesus that you may charge certain persons not to teach any different doctrine, nor to occupy themselves with myths and endless genealogies which promote speculations rather than the divine training that is in faith" (1:4). This is followed by a warning about certain persons who have "wandered away into vain discussion, desiring to be teachers of the law, without understanding either what they are saying or the things about which they make assertions" (vv. 6-7).

Timothy's mentor in the work of the ministry added weight to a point made earlier, concerning the multiple functions of apostles, when he spoke of having been "ordained a preacher, and an apostle . . . a teacher [*didas-*

kalos] of the Gentiles in faith and verity" (1 Tim. 2:7, KJV).

As in the letter to Titus, 1 Timothy 3:1 says that a bishop must be "apt to teach" (KJV); and Timothy was urged to "attend to the public reading of scripture, to preaching, to teaching [*didaskalia*]" (4:13).

In a passage somewhat reminiscent of the instruction to Titus concerning the "older women" (Titus 2:3-4) who teach younger women, 2 Timothy 2:2 says, "And what you have heard from me before many witnesses entrust to faithful men who will be able to teach others also." Does this mean that Timothy, along with his other pastoral duties, was responsible for training other teachers in the church?

A preacher-teacher must handle the Word which has been entrusted to him with fidelity and accuracy. This is the point of 2 Timothy 2:15. The exhortation to handle the Word of truth rightly is reinforced by the verse which follows: "Avoid such godless chatter, for it will lead people into more and more ungodliness" (v. 16).

The exhortation, "preach the word," from 2 Timothy 4:2, has served as the theme for many ordination sermons. But the verse also speaks of other forms of communication ("convincing," "rebuking," "exhorting," and "teaching") in addition to preaching. Here is further evidence that the pastor during the New Testament era typically functioned as a teacher.

What we see in the Pastorals is a church in which the teaching role was more formalized than it was at an earlier period. Those who served in pastoral roles were the chief teachers. But they also were trainers and overseers of other teachers, such as the "faithful men" mentioned in 2 Timothy and the "older women" referred to in Titus. Apparently, a growing concern for fidelity to the Word was generated by a proliferation of false teachers during this period.

And this points up the fact that teachers are obligated to be faithful to truth, and not to lapse into error through ignorance or self-serving attitudes.

The High Calling

Nowhere in Scripture is the gravity of the teaching task spelled out more clearly than in James 3:1: "Let not many of you become teachers, my brethren, for you know that we who teach shall be judged with greater strictness."

Strong language this and not very palatable to those who tend to be casual about teaching. And it is not likely to be publicized widely by religious educators who find it difficult enough to staff Sunday School positions with warm bodies, even without scaring willing prospects away with such dire warnings.

The King James Version's "be not many masters" tends to obscure the meaning of the passage for modern readers who aren't accustomed to calling teachers "master," as they did in seventeenth-century England. The Greek term *didaskaloi* meant "teachers." So the biblical writer's warning is not addressed to people who want to lord it over others; it is directed to those who aspire to teach. And the message must be taken at face value: "Think twice before becoming a teacher; for teachers will be judged very strictly."

Why should the judgment of teachers be so stringent? Perhaps it is because teachers are in a position to do

144 Why the Church Must Teach

maximum damage if they err. An individual can pervert truth without harming anyone but himself. But a false teacher can multiply error a hundred times over.

This interpretation is supported by other Scriptures which hint at a problem of increasing proportions during the New Testament era—a widespread proliferation of unqualified and unworthy teachers.

James 3:1 could quite appropriately be applied to the "certain persons" mentioned in 1 Timothy 1:6-7, who "have wandered away into vain discussion, desiring to be teachers of the law, without understanding either what they are saying or the things about which they make assertions."

2 Timothy 4:3 warns that "the time is coming when people will not endure sound teaching, but having itching ears they will accumulate for themselves teachers to suit their own likings."

And, in his poignant farewell to the Ephesian elders at Miletus (Acts 20), Paul warned against certain "fierce wolves" who would come in to devour the congregation by "speaking perverse things, to draw away disciples after them" (vv. 29-30).

These and other Scriptures convey the distinct impression that the church was overrun with would-be teachers who were unqualified or inspired by self-serving motives. Perhaps some of these were sincere; but lacking the gift of teaching, they failed to meet the high standards by which teachers were measured. Others were insincere pretenders, posing as teachers for personal gain or self-aggrandizement. In either case, they could do great damage to the cause of Christ.

The teacher's vocation was regarded with utmost seriousness in the New Testament period and with good reason. As custodian of Christian tradition, the teacher was responsible for a message which was not his own but was, in the final analysis, the Word of God. Such a message must be taught with unswerving fidelity. As interpreter of tradition, the teacher was also a *maker* of tradition. Any distortion of truth would not only mislead his immediate hearers but could also contaminate tradition for generations to come.

Teaching as Calling: A Summary

The God of the Bible is a teaching God. From the beginning he has sought to reveal his will to humankind through intelligible symbols designed to take root in the human mind. And from the beginning, God has commissioned teachers to be co-workers in this task. The parents, priests, prophets, and sages of the Hebrew nation functioned as teachers, under the mandate of the Teacher of Israel.

In the New Testament, Jesus was first and foremost a teacher. He commissioned his disciples to go into all the world—teaching. But, even as the Lord was always considered to be the true Educator of Israel, Jesus Christ continued to be the Teacher of the church, through the work of the Paraclete. He modeled teaching in his earthly ministry. He provided the curriculum for teaching in the early church. And he equipped those who were chosen to teach through endowing them with spiritual gifts.

All of these co-workers in the educational mission—parents, priests, prophets, apostles, pastors, and teachers—shared a deep sense of divine calling. Careful examination of the biblical record shows that God always initiated the teaching function, provided the message to be taught, selected coteachers, and prepared them for the task.

As it was then, so it is today. The teaching function of the church still grows out of the divine initiative. The Lord still calls men and women to this task. It is much too crucial to leave to casual or grudging volunteers. The enlistment of teachers in the church today should be predicated on the assumption that the Spirit still summons teachers into service and gives them the gifts needed for the task. This applies not only to "professional" ministers but to "lay" leadership as well.

Christian teaching will once again regain the preeminence it enjoyed in the New Testament period when churches come to regard the selection of teachers as "calling out the called," rather than a coaxing of the recalcitrant.

Notes

1. Lewis J. Sherrill, *The Rise of Christian Education* (New York: The Macmillan Co., 1944), p. 21.

2. Ibid., p. 158.

3. Francis Brown, S. R. Driver, and Charles A. Briggs, eds., *A Hebrew and English Lexicon of the Old Testament* (Oxford: Clarendon Press, 1974), p. 612.

4. Max Salomon, "Education," Isaac Landman, ed., *The Universal Jewish Encyclopedia* (New York: The Universal Jewish Encyclopedia, Inc., 1941), Vol. 3, p. 629.

5. Robert W. Henderson, *The Teaching Office in the Reformed Tradition: A History of the Doctoral Ministry* (Philadelphia: The Westminster Press, 1962), p. 27.

6. Floyd V. Filson, "The Christian Teacher in the First Century," *Journal of Biblical Literature,* 60 (1941), p. 322.

7. The authority for this interpretation of *noutheteo* is J. Behm, *"noutheteo,"* Gerhard Kittel, ed., *Theological Dictionary of the New Testament* (Grand Rapids, MI: William B. Eerdmans Publishing Co., 1967), Vol. IV, pp. 1019-22.

8. Raymond B. Brown, "1 Corinthians," *The Broadman Bible Commentary* (Nashville: Broadman Press, 1970), Vol. 10, p. 362*f.*

9. James D. G. Dunn, *Jesus and the Spirit* (London: SCM Press Ltd., 1975), p. 283.

10. Ralph P. Martin, "Ephesians," *The Broadman Bible Commentary* (Nashville: Broadman Press, 1971), Vol. 11, p. 156.

11. Dunn, Ibid.

8
Why the Church Must Teach Today

Teaching is an essential function within the Christian community, just as metabolic processes are vital to a living organism. Teaching may take place in worship services, Bible classes, counseling sessions, training events, choir rehearsals, and Christian homes. But it *must* take place.

Why? Because, as James Smart once pointed out:

> The Church must teach, just as it must preach, or it will not be the Church. . . . Teaching belongs to the essence of the Church and a church that neglects this function of teaching has lost something that is indispensable to its nature as a church.[1]

Teaching and a Church's Identity

A sobering warning appears in the letter to the Ephesian church, recorded in Revelation 2:5. The Lord says: "Remember then from what you have fallen, repent and do the works you did at first. If not, I will come to you and remove your lampstand from its place, unless you repent."

These words suggest the horrifying possibility that a

congregation can actually lose its identity as a church of the Lord Jesus Christ, perhaps without even knowing it. They might go on meeting weekly in a building with stained-glass windows and a steeple. They might have a sign over the doorway which says CHURCH. They might carry out all the weekly meetings and rituals which we have learned to associate with churches, and yet cease to be a church in the eyes of God.

What exactly makes a church a church? What is the difference between a church and any other collection of human beings?

One of the defining characteristics of a church is its obedience to the Word of God as revealed through Jesus Christ, recorded in the Scriptures, interpreted by the Holy Spirit, and affirmed by Christian tradition. The church was brought into being by the self-revelation of God in Jesus Christ (John 1:14; Heb. 1:1-2). This is not just a theological proposition, it is a historical datum. The church which appeared in Jerusalem following the resurrection would not have come into existence apart from the Word as revealed in the life and teachings of Jesus. Just as Israel had been born of the Word which God communicated to Moses on Sinai, so the New Israel was born of the Word which was incarnated in the second Moses (John 1:17; Acts 3:22).

In the historical narratives of the New Testament, the same pattern always prevailed. The communication of the Word through preaching and teaching invariably preceded the founding of new congregations. And in our own day, churches are always planted in the seedbed of the preached and the taught Word of God. Every congregation owes its existence to the shared Word of God.

But it would be equally valid to say that a church *maintains* its existence by the Word of God. A church is often defined as "a body of baptized believers." But a church is not merely that. A church is a congregation of the people of God who, having entered into a saving relationship with Christ, live in continuous obedience to his Word. The corporate identity of a church is analogous to the individual identity of a single disciple of Jesus Christ.

The first duty of a disciple is to follow the one who has called him. This entails not only an initial response but also continuing obedience to the Master's bidding. It requires not only an expression of willingness to follow but a day by day walk in the way of the Master as well. If one does not continue in the Master's Word, he is no longer his disciple (John 8:31). To call Jesus Lord and not do the things he has said would be paradoxical (Luke 6:46), for his lordship assumes followship.

And so it is with a church. A church is a band of disciples who continue in his Word. To say that Christ is head of the church, while denying the necessity of obedience to his Word, is contradictory and nonsensical.

But continuing in his Word presupposes an understanding of his Word, and such understanding comes neither automatically nor cheaply. Understanding of his Word is purchased only at the price of faithful study and diligent application. Anyone who is tempted to think otherwise should be reminded that even those first disciples who sat daily at the feet of the Master were slow to grasp the meaning of his teaching. For example, even after Simon Peter's inspired confession at Caesarea Philippi ("You are the Christ"), this same disciple rebuked

Jesus for speaking of the suffering that he must undergo (Matt. 16:22-23), thus betraying a serious lack of understanding of Jesus' messianic mission. Even after the resurrection, there was still uncertainty concerning the Lord's messianic role (Acts 1:6), though he had repeatedly revealed to him his intention to become a spiritual, rather than a political, messiah.

Remember too how frequently the writers of New Testament epistles found it necessary to urge the Christians of their generation to grow in their knowledge of Jesus Christ (1 Pet. 2:2; 2 Pet. 3:18); to leave the "elementary doctrines of Christ and go on to maturity (Heb. 6:1); and to "grow up" in Christ (Eph. 4:11-13). They were cautioned not to be naive like "children tossed to and fro and carried about with every wind of [teaching]" (Eph. 4:14), to be on guard against perversions of the gospel (Gal. 1:6-7).

Contemporary Christians who insist that an experience of regeneration makes further study of the Word of God unnecessary are either ignorant of, or indifferent to, this New Testament evidence. If first-generation Christians who were closest to the earthly ministry of Jesus did not attain instant understanding of his teachings, how much more do we, separated from that event by nearly 2,000 years, need to continue in a ceaseless effort to understand the words of our Lord.

The conditions which prompted warnings against false teachings, spiritual immaturity, and misunderstandings of Scripture during the New Testament era are equally appropriate today, because the conditions which prompted those warnings are very much with us.

Where Christian teaching and learning are neglected,

the Word of God becomes contaminated with current folk beliefs, cultural values, superstitions, political doctrines, secular philosophies, and personal prejudices. Many church members in our time are more conversant with paperback books on demonology, astrology, and ancient godlike astronauts than they are with the Scriptures. Well-intentioned Christians give cash contributions to door-to-door peddlers of cleverly camouflaged heresy because they are not well enough informed to discriminate between truth and error.

One summer afternoon at a religious conference center, I listened to a bizarre tale about a church that had virtually been destroyed by ignorance. For more than two hours, a distressed lady described the capture of her home church by a cunning preacher who seemed obsessed by a strange combination of spiritualism and demonology. "I can look a person in the eye and tell how many demons he has in him," the preacher had boasted from the pulpit. Before the church had finally fallen apart, high schoolers were "sacrificing" the tips of fingers to the devil, two women had been committed to mental institutions, and a band of the preacher's supporters had covenanted together to pray for the deaths of those who opposed him. As I listened in stunned silence, the woman concluded her extraordinary story by saying, "This would not have happened if the people in our church had not been so ignorant of the Word of God."

Her church had lost its identity, and she had lost her church. The experience of that congregation makes one of Smart's observations glow with unusual relevance:

The peril of the Church is always from within. If it is

the Church of God, rightly hearing God's Word to it in the gospel, and responding to it with an unconditional faith, there is no power in all the earth that can destroy it. It does not need to fear its adversaries, however powerful they may be. But let it become something other than the Church of God in itself and at once it is vulnerable to its enemies. . . . The enemy from without has power to destroy the Church only when he finds the Church confused in its faith, vague concerning its own nature and destiny, and no longer clear in its own mind about what it owes to either God or man.[2]

Failure to live in obedience to the Word of God does not always grow out of a spirit of rebellion. It might just as surely stem from a lack of knowledge, for people cannot obey what they do not understand. There is a disobedience born of ignorance when failure to act stems from failure to know.

When the function of teaching is neglected within a church, the congregation will eventually develop spiritual amnesia, forgetting who under God they are supposed to be. The result is that the church gradually becomes homogenized with the secular society surrounding her, languishing in a pattern of cultural sameness, undifferentiated and innocuous.

Smart speaks of the need for a discipline in which the church will "mount the watchtower and scan its life and faith in all directions, in order to detect the presence of blindness, unbelief, unfaithfulness, and sin, and give warning before it is too late."[3] He is speaking of the task of theology. Not book-bound theology in the abstract, but a living theology that might better be described as "theologizing." "Theology," Smart says, "is simply the

Church taking with complete seriousness the question of its own existence and inquiring with the utmost thoroughness at what points it is failing to be the Church of God."⁴

Teaching and Christian Tradition

A church's continuing quest for identity involves faithful communication of tradition. "Tradition" is not a popular word among some Christians. To them the term seems somewhat unspiritual, since it is laden with negative connotations in some New Testament passages (for example, Matt. 15:2-3, 6; Col. 2:8). In fact, our generation as a whole is not on very friendly terms with tradition. To many of our contemporaries in this hyped-up age, the word *tradition* sounds squeaky and antiquated.

Admittedly, tradition can become cankerous and stale when it outlasts its reason for being. In fact, when tradition has nothing to prop it up except that tired old crutch, "That's how we've always done it," it can become positively annoying. But that is tradition at its worst. Tradition at its best is the distilled essence of wisdom and experience which one generation carefully passes on to the next, just as the coals from colonial hearths were passed from one home to another in the deadly chill of New England winters. And tradition is just that indispensable to the church.

Christian tradition consists of the doctrines, values, customs, rituals, and historical data which contribute to the ongoing experience, and thus to the corporate identity, of the body.

For many years after the death and resurrection of Jesus, his teachings were carefully communicated from person to person, from church to church, in the form of oral tradition. When Paul wrote to the Corinthians, "For I delivered to you as of first importance what I also received" (1 Cor. 15:3), he was referring to the tradition (*paradosis*) which had been passed on to him as a novice in the faith.

At the beginning of what probably is the New Testament's earliest account of the institution of the Lord's Supper, Paul wrote, "For I received from the Lord what I also delivered to you" (1 Cor. 11:23). This reference illustrates the important point that early Christian tradition was intimately associated with the Lord himself. This was true for two reasons. In the first place, the church's tradition was rooted in the sayings of Jesus. The Lord had originated the chain of tradition. But, beyond that, the Lord was still at work in the church as interpreter of the tradition.

Cullmann has suggested that early Christian tradition (*paradosis*) consisted of three elements:

> First, rules which after the fashion of the *halacha* [Jewish rules of conduct] have to do with the conduct of the faithful, as for example 1 Cor. 11.2; 2 Thess. 3.6; Rom. 6.17; Phil. 4.9; Col. 2.6; secondly, a summary of the Christian preaching, fixed after the fashion of a rule of faith, where facts of the life of Jesus are united with their theological interpretation, as in 1 Cor. 15.3ff.; finally, words and single narratives from the life of Jesus, as in 1 Cor. 11.23.[5]

If this is the meaning of tradition, it is obvious that the church cannot neglect it without soon becoming theologically, spiritually, and morally bankrupt.

The church must handle Christian tradition with one foot planted firmly in history and the other resting on Christ's promise of the continual guidance of the Spirit. The early Christians in Thessalonica were exhorted to "hold the traditions" which they had been taught (2 Thess. 2:15). And so must we. If we do not, we will become a cut-flower generation of churchgoers, doctrinally rootless entrepreneurs of a faddish religion. New ideas and interpretations must always be tested for their congruence with the testimony of the Scriptures, the primary documents of our faith.

On the other hand, we must teach the ancient story with eyes and ears attuned to the Holy Spirit who will "lead us into all truth" as we seek to relate a living gospel to new and changing situations. Both aspects of this task are within the special province of the church's teaching function.

But the task of communicating Christian tradition is not confined to the church building itself. Let it be remembered that Paul exhorted parents to train their children in the traditions which they cherished as members of the community of faith (Eph. 6:4). This responsibility belongs in a special way to parents. The opportunities for instructing children within the context of daily family living cannot be equaled anywhere else in the world. Sunday School is a vitally important experience for children, but it will never take the place of Christian nurture in the home. As parents teach children to pray at mealtime, comment on God's goodness as provider of peanut butter and jelly sandwiches, share simple Bible stories at bedtime, and, most important, model Christlike conduct in human relations, they function as teachers of Christian tradition. And this is a telling argument for adult education in the church, for parents cannot share with their children what they themselves do not know.

The teaching of tradition within the church facilitates participation in the life of the congregation and engenders a sense of continuity with the people of God through every generation. It includes studies in Christian history, church polity, and training in worship practices. It also includes biblical tradition—the stories of the heroes of the faith, the great events of biblical history, the poetry of the Psalms, the teachings of Jesus, and the exciting narratives concerning the work of the early church. Some religious educators, swayed by the tenets of progressive education, are reluctant to teach biblical material which does not have immediate application to life situations. But a large body of biblical information should be taught by the church, in the classroom and from the pulpit, simply because it is essential to basic schooling in the faith. The modern notion that one may be thoroughly Christian, though biblically illiterate, finds little support in the Bible itself.

On repeated occasions, all the members of the congregation become teachers as they act out their traditions in worship services, fellowship events, ministry projects, and church business sessions. The church's periodic celebration of the Lord's Supper is a prime example.

One Sunday evening, as our church observed this memorial supper by candlelight, a nine-year-old boy sat beside me. He had started attending church services only recently, and this was a strange, new experience for him. As the bread was being distributed, he asked, "What are they doing?" Later, as the cup was passed from person to person, he inquired, "What are they doing now?" What a joy it was to share with him the meaning of one of our most cherished traditions.

Teaching and Evangelism

From the beginning, the church has lived under the divine mandate, "Ye shall be witnesses unto me" (Acts 1:8, KJV). Since the function of a witness is to tell what he has seen and heard, it seems evident that the primary qualification of a Christian witness is a first-hand experience with Christ. But, in addition, an effective witness also knows how to articulate the meaning of his experience. Dog-paddling around in a pool of religious words is a poor way to attract potential disciples.

How impressed I was when, in the early 1970s, I saw television films of "Jesus freaks" out on the streets of American cities bearing witness to their faith. But how disappointed I was when I had my first face-to-face encounter with one of these young people on a Hollywood street corner. He was a Bible-totin' robot, programmed to emit an indecipherable stream of religious gibberish. No matter how my Christian companion and I responded, he kept playing the same tape, a mixture of foreboding prophecies, warnings about the demon world, and tattered fragments of gospel thrown in for good measure.

This is not to suggest that this young man was typical of "Jesus freaks." I am simply making the point that a muddled gospel can be more confusing than helpful, no matter how sincere the intentions behind it. Here was a demonstration of faith, courage, and zeal—all admirable

traits in any evangelist, but immeasurably more meaningful when accompanied by knowledge and reason.

And this is precisely where the teaching ministry inter-
faces with the church's evangelistic task in the preparation of witnesses. In the first place, Christian instruction
offers believers the opportunity to crystallize the meaning of their experience in Christ, just as Saul of Tarsus did
during those days in Damascus after he had met the risen
Lord on the road from Jerusalem (Acts 9:8-19). Second,
it helps modern-day disciples find workable answers to
that difficult question, How do you tell modern man that
'Jesus saves'? Encoding the old, old story into twentieth-
century thought forms requires persistence, wisdom, and
insight. Third, Christian teaching provides biblical resources for the work of evangelism. A striking characteristic of New Testament evangelists was the consistency
with which they used their knowledge of the Scriptures
to get the gospel message across. And this same resource
is essential to the church's evangelistic mission today.

In addition to these linkages between the church's
educational and evangelistic functions, it should also be
pointed out that teaching often becomes a front-line
evangelistic strategy. Bible study sessions in jails and
prisons, on college campuses, at neighborhood coffee
klatches, in medical centers, and in apartment complexes
have proven to be effective vehicles for communicating
the gospel in our generation.

Christians from many walks of life are providing leadership for this venture in educational evangelism. At
UCLA, a professor of dentistry convenes a weekly Bible
study group in his office. A group of laymen in Louisville,
Kentucky, meet for Bible study and prayer at a local

restaurant one morning each week. In Houston, Texas, large numbers of single adults gather for Bible study in local cafeterias during lunch breaks. A group of Christian women in Memphis, Tennessee, bring neighbors and other acquaintances to the home of their Sunday School teacher for weekday Bible study.

This approach to discipling has exciting potential. But it requires knowledgeable, disciplined leadership. Biblical illiteracy and personal incompetence at the helm of such study groups can only have a damaging effect. The teaching evangelists who invest themselves in this enterprise must turn to their churches for training, since few of them will have opportunities for training of this kind anywhere else. Their churches must become seminaries for lay ministers.

Paul undoubtedly had something like this in mind when he spelled out the purpose of spiritual gifts in Ephesians 4:11-12. In this passage he suggests that one of the primary reasons for the presence of apostles, prophets, evangelists, and pastor-teachers in the church is to "prepare God's people for works of service" (v. 12, NIV). Translated into contemporary terms, this means that the most highly-skilled teachers in the church ought to serve as coaches, preparing others to function as teacher-evangelists.

Teaching and Worship

Some people want a worship experience devoid of intellectual content, an inspirational exercise that warms the heart without affecting the head. They expect worship services to provide an escape from thinking, to afford euphoric relief from the heavy burden of revealed truth. Such a person was the woman who, at the conclusion of a sermon on the relationship between Christian love and social problems, said to her pastor reprovingly, "I come to church to get away from the problems of the world, not to be reminded of them."

Worshipers of this stripe sing about a holy God without ever wondering what true holiness is. They repeat the "Lord's Prayer" without having the foggiest notion what it would mean if the kingdom really did come. Perhaps this is worship, but it is not Christian worship. It is worship at the Athenian altar inscribed, "To an unknown God" (Acts 17:23).

One seminary student conducted a survey among adults in her home church, asking a single question: "In a brief paragraph, tell what you believe about God." This was an affluent congregation in which men and women were generally well-educated. Yet many of their responses were shockingly naive. Some described God as a supreme being whose dwelling place was "the sky." More than a few said, in so many words, that God loves us "when he is pleased" with our lives. One man, generally regarded as one of the "faithful members" of the church, said he hadn't given the subject much thought.

The question is, Can a person who "doesn't give the subject much thought" worship the true and living God, the God of the Bible?

I was once told by a person who resides in Mexico that when the Spanish conquistadors went into that country they encouraged native Indians to worship at their Christian altars by placing local idols behind the altars. Whether or not that story is historically authentic, it does illustrate the point I want to make here. Is it possible that when congregations assemble for Christian worship, some individuals are worshiping images conjured up in their own minds, rather than the God who has revealed himself through Jesus Christ, the "Word made flesh"?

When the choirs of Israel sang their psalms in the Temple, there was no doubt about the identity of the God whom they worshiped. Theirs was no abstract deity. He was the "God of Abraham" (Ps. 47:9), the "God of Jacob" (Ps. 46:7), the God of Joseph's kin (Ps. 80:1), the "Shepherd of Israel." His mighty deeds in the history of the nation were sung again and again (Pss. 77, 78, 105). There was a distinctive didactic element in these liturgies, and this alliance between teachings *about* God and the worship *of* God was carried over into the synagogue service at a later date.

The church must teach because teaching is an indispensable concomitant of worship. Teaching without worship is a dead intellectual exercise, but worship without teaching always teeters on the brink of idolatry. Ignorance of the revealed God can only result in worship of an imagined god.

Early Christian congregational meetings followed a pattern similar to that of the synagogue, combining instruction with worship. In the primitive church, the Christian meeting which most nearly resembled today's worship services was the "meeting for the Word." Sherrill has identified six elements which seem to have been included in such a service: (1) *Prayer,* offered by any member of the congregation who felt led to pray. (2) *Psalms and hymns and spiritual songs.* These were considered a way of "admonishing one another" and "speaking one to another." (3) *The reading of apostolic letters,* when these were available. (4) *A Didache,* a teaching, based on the Hebrew Scriptures, the sayings of Jesus, and Christian traditions concerning faith and conduct. (5) *The prophecy.* Prophetic utterances were regarded as given by the Spirit, and might come from various members of the congregation. (6) *"Speaking with tongues,"* an aspect of early Christian worship which was permitted, but not encouraged, by Paul (1 Cor. 14:2-19).[6] (This practice is not mentioned in later New Testament writings.)

When one compares today's church services with early Christian worship, one wonders whatever happened to the educational emphasis which was such a vital part of those first-century congregational meetings. The element of worship which most nearly approximated the modern sermon was the *Didache.* This, apparently, was the only prepared public discourse delivered by an individual to the congregation. And the *Didache* was clearly regarded as a teaching event—an exposition of Scripture, the sayings of Jesus, or some Christian tradition. The crackerjack homilies and promotional pep talks so often delivered from modern pulpits are a far cry from the didactic messages heard by those first Christian congregations. Only genuinely expository preaching can approach the instructional quality of those edifying discourses.

Teaching and Christian Conduct

The earliest Christians were known as followers of "the Way" (Acts 9:2; 19:9, 23; 22:4; 24:14, 22). And, indeed, they were. They were not only distinguished by their beliefs, they were also known for the way they lived. They lived by an ethic of love which stood over against the callousness and debauchery of a pagan culture. And many members of their secular society saw the quality of their lives, and believed.

Commenting on this point, T. W. Manson once wrote:

> The Christianity that conquered the Roman Empire was not an affair of brilliant preachers addressing packed congregations. We have, so far as I know, nothing much in the way of brilliant preachers in the first three hundred years of the Church's life. . . . The great preachers came after Constantine the Great; and before that Christianity had already done its work and made its way right through the Empire from end to end. When we try to picture how it was done we seem to see domestic servants teaching Christ in and through their domestic service, workers doing it through their work, small shopkeepers through their trade, and so on, rather than eloquent propagandists swaying mass meetings of interested inquirers.[7]

Manson went on to say something else that is highly relevant to the church's teaching task today:

> It is still true that the best propaganda for genuine Christianity is genuine Christians; and the New Testament is full of declarations of the convincing power, not of the spoken word, but of the lived life. Indeed, I think it is fair to say that the lives of Christians will have to be the parables of the Kingdom for the twentieth century.[8]

If the lives of Christians do serve as "parables of the Kingdom" in our generation, it will be, in part, because they have been taught how to live in "the Way." To be sure, the dynamic of the Christian life is the transforming power of the indwelling Christ (2 Cor. 5:17). But the direction of the Christian life has always been a primary concern of the teaching ministry. Never in the New

Testament is it assumed that a person acquires a comprehensive knowledge of proper conduct at conversion. Having received eternal life, converts must be taught how to live. In Ephesians 4:17-32, for example, there is a long discourse which focuses on the subject of proper Christian conduct. After speaking of the pagan Gentiles, who have "given themselves up to licentiousness, greedy to practice every kind of uncleanness" (v. 19), the writer said to his Christian readers, "You did not so learn Christ!—assuming that you have heard about him and were taught in him" (vv. 20-21). What follows is a list of instructions for Christian living.

Instruction in ethical conduct was a continuing need in the early church as the Christian gospel encountered new situations. The rule of love was in constant need of reinterpretation as Christians wrestled with social issues, such as the relationship of slave to master, the Christian's role in military service, and the problem of marriages in which believers were "unequally yoked" to nonbelievers.

And that need is no less pressing in our day. In an increasingly secularized age, Christians are called upon to live G-rated lives in an X-rated world, dealing with a multiplicity of new issues brought on by technological and social change. For example, what should be a Christian's stance toward a mass media environment in which there are no more taboos to be broken? No known category of human perversion has escaped the descriptive pen and the probing lens. Illicit sexual behavior is omnipresent in books, newspapers, magazines, and pop music; it permeates television programming and even commercial advertising. Pornography is legitimized; adultery is glorified; and homosexuality is presented casually as a matter of personal preference.

How should Christians respond to yesterday's science fiction concepts which have become today's realities through medical science—artificial insemination, *in vitrio* fertilization, surrogate motherhood, and human cloning? And should a Christian consider buying a kidney from someone willing to sell it, if it becomes a matter of life and death?

There is evidence that "the Way" sometimes becomes obscure for modern-day disciples. A minister whose church is near a state university told of having received a telephone call from one of his parishioners, a twenty-year-old coed. She was debating whether or not to move in with her fiance during their last year of college, "to save money for the wedding," and wondered what her pastor thought of the idea. "The thing that shocked me," he later said to a group of fellow ministers, "is not that a college student would consider such a thing, but that she really didn't know what my attitude would be."

These are but a few of the ethical issues confronting contemporary Christianity. Paul's problem concerning meat offered to idols (1 Cor. 8) has in our day turned into a complex array of moral dilemmas. The church must teach, because Christians are still seeking to walk in "the Way," and the world is still waiting to see whether or not Christ makes a difference.

Informed Christians in a Technological World

As the twentieth century draws to a close, it becomes increasingly important for the people of God to know who they are and to be able to communicate their faith convincingly. This is because they must live and work in a technological culture where the greatest threat to the church is not persecution but assimilation.

Technology is not just automated machinery, plastic gimmickry, and electric circuitry. It is a way of thinking —a disciplined, systematic approach to the solving of problems, including those problems which were once relegated to religion. It is analytical and logical, and is opposed to intuitive, aesthetic, and mystical modes of thought.

Technological man is not necessarily antagonistic toward religion. He is more inclined to see it as a resource for encouraging people to think high and noble thoughts and to perpetuate useful sentiments. He invites the church to become a part of the religio-cultural dimension of society, providing "metaphysics-in-a-God-key," as Stendahl once phrased it.[9] This would, of course, amount to a serious subversion of the church's prophetic role.

If Christians are to take that role seriously, they must know who they are in contradistinction to the world which surrounds them. If they are to communicate the gospel effectively, they must know what they are talking about. Never before in American Christianity has there been a more urgent need for the church to develop informed, thinking men and women who know how to rightly divide the word of truth, discriminate between biblical revelation and popular folklore, and who have the holy audacity to live out an incarnational faith in a secularized society.

This is most likely to happen in congregations where teaching-learning activity flourishes, where members partake of the spirit of inquiry that motivated those noble

Bereans who "received the word with all readiness of mind, and searched the scriptures daily, whether those things were so" (Acts 17:11, KJV).

A vital teaching ministry invites a congregation to engage in continuous exploration of the Word which called them into being as a community of believers. "Exploration" is a fitting term, for, in its most elemental sense, the verb "explore" does not refer to private investigation or solitary searching. Rather, it denotes the communication activity of persons who "call out" to one another as they make discoveries related to their common quest.

Notes

1. James D. Smart, *The Teaching Ministry of the Church* (Philadelphia: The Westminster Press, 1954), p. 11.
2. Ibid., p. 33.
3. Ibid., p. 32*f.*
4. Ibid., p. 33.
5. Oscar Cullmann, " 'KYRIOS' as Designation for the Oral Tradition Concerning Jesus," *Scottish Journal of Theology,* Vol. 3 (June 1950), No. 2, p. 186.
6. Lewis J. Sherrill, *The Rise of Christian Education* (New York: The Macmillan Co., 1944), pp. 153-56.
7. T. W. Manson, *Ministry and Priesthood* (Richmond, VA: John Knox Press, n.d.), p. 21.
8. Ibid.
9. Krister Stendahl, "Religion, Mysticism, and the Institutional Church," *Daedalus,* (Summer 1967), p. 856.